The McGraw-Hill Handbook of
Business
Letters

Roy W. Poe

FOURTH EDITION

McGraw-Hill, Inc.

New York Chicago San Francisco Lisbon
London Madrid Mexico City Milan New Delhi
San Juan Seoul Singapore Sydney Toronto

Contents

Part 4   CREDIT AND COLLECTION LETTERS / 99

Part 5   MORE SAMPLE LETTERS / 119

Contents

Introduction

Over the years, a lot of fuss has been made about the high cost of business communications. When you consider costs like stationery, postage, overhead, and the writer's time, the cost of a single letter can be astronomical. Although e-mail is faster, each e-mail still represents an investment in equipment, time, and money.

But let's be realistic. The dollars *spent* to put a letter in the mail can be inconsequential when compared to the dollars *lost* by writing a bad letter—or no letter at all. A terse message to a highly valued customer might be economical, but it could result in less business. If so, that message was a very expensive "economical" letter.

Business communications are substitutes for face-to-face visits, making and keeping friends, attracting and holding customers, and building a favorable image for your company. Effective business writing helps promote long-term relationships with customers and, ultimately, leads to greater profits.

This fourth edition of *The McGraw-Hill Handbook of Business Letters* has the same goal as previous editions—to offer samples of effective business communications. A wide variety of business situations are covered—from asking for special favors to saying no with the least possible offense.

Because of new technology, business communications have changed dramatically. Most routine written communications are via e-mail. More formal communications, such as important letters, proposals, and contracts, are expedited using faxes and next-day delivery services. Voice mail, IMs (Instant Messages), and teleconferences are used to maintain personal contact when one or more persons are not immediately available for face-to-face conversations.

In keeping with previous editions, the examples in this book are shown in the traditional business letter format. However, each of these could be sent as an e-mail, memo, or other form of written business communication. The format might change, but the message remains the same.

The McGraw-Hill Handbook of
Business Letters

Part 1

THE BUSINESS WRITER'S CRAFT

Effective Business Letters Make a Difference

A letter may be thought of as a substitute for a personal visit. It is not possible for us to meet and talk with everyone with whom we want to communicate—whether distant friends, fellow employees just three floors or one building away, or clients and suppliers scattered everywhere. Even the telephone is not always a satisfactory means of communicating.

Even if we could handle all our business and social communications on a face-to-face basis, however, we would still need to prepare written communications. For one thing, we often need a permanent record of what was said, to whom, by whom, and on what date. For another, written communications often do a better job than the spoken word.

There are many reasons for needing to write effective business communications. First, your value to your organization will be greatly enhanced if you can share information and exchange ideas efficiently and successfully. Your ability to communicate well often means faster progress up the promotion ladder. Competent writers are not as plentiful as one might imagine, and those who can write well always stand out.

Second, those who can compose effective business letters make new friends and keep old ones for the organization, thereby increasing sales and profits, which all businesses need for survival.

Third, good writers can save time and effort for their companies. A great deal of money is wasted each year by people who write windy and garbled messages that befuddle and exhaust their readers.

Finally, your rating as an employee—which hinges greatly on your skill in working harmoniously with the people around you—rises dramatically when you master the art of writing sensible, tactful, and finely honed communications.

What Is Good Business Writing?

A good business letter is one that obtains the results the writer hoped for. Of course, we're assuming that writers want what is best for (1) the organizations they work for and (2) the individuals to whom the letters are addressed.

Good business letters are not too long—usually one page. They are tactful, courteous, clear, conversational, personal, and interesting. Every business letter is also a sales letter. You're selling a product, a company image, an idea, or yourself.

These are rules for ideal conditions, and as we know, business conditions are rarely ideal. We all prefer to work where harmony and good cheer prevail, because surliness and bickering affect employee attitudes as well as productivity. If you're answering an inquiry from a potential customer who is genuinely interested in your company's products, you're off and running. Your letter is friendly, tactful, personal, courteous, sales-structured, and the rest.

But what if you're a credit manager and you have to write a sixth letter to a longtime customer who appears to have no intention of paying the $4,000 that is now six months past due? Here you have to try something different. Now you're going to write a "pay or else" letter that will sound about as friendly as a wounded grizzly.

Just as we know that letters are rarely nasty and gruff, we also know that good letters are not necessarily joyous either. In our own daily dealings with people, we sometimes have strong differences of opinion, some individuals are cranky and unreasonable, and tempers can flare when dumb mistakes generate agonizing crises. Employees are pressured to improve their performance, increase profits, and improve productivity.

Thus, effective business writing means that we're striving to keep friends, generate goodwill, and enhance sales opportunities.

Good letters can be hard to write, simply because readers are so different. Even circumstances can affect the reaction you receive. For example, something goes wrong, it's your fault, and two customers are affected. You write a beautifully crafted letter of apology to both of them.

Customer A's response is very pleasant. You are relieved because the reaction you got was exactly what you'd hoped for.

Thanks for letting me know. The situation was understandable; we make our share of mistakes, too.

Yet Customer B responds negatively. This is not the reaction you want.

I'm fed up. Your explanation isn't good enough. I've lost money because of you, and I'm taking my business elsewhere.

How is it possible to win and lose with the same letter? The two recipients and/or circumstances may be entirely different. Customer A may have had plenty of stock in the warehouse and was not overly inconvenienced by getting the wrong merchandise. Or he may be a longtime satisfied customer with several personal friends in the company. Or he may owe you a favor for a special service in the past. Or perhaps he's just a person who doesn't rile easily.

Customer B, in contrast, may own a small business with a limited inventory, so any delay in getting the right merchandise could be disastrous. Or he may be a new customer who has placed only a few orders, all of which were fouled up. Or he may be a person with a short fuse who is overworked and harried.

So business writing is a very personal process. Communications are written by and to people, and the content of a particular message depends on how writers feel about their subject, how well they know their readers, and what attitudes and policies are set by the organizations they represent.

Imagine a popular speaker addressing a large convention. A dozen or so audience members are impressed enough to write to her about her talk. Although the letters will have some common characteristics—complimentary, tactful, friendly, and so on—no two will be exactly alike. They will vary in approach, length, and emphasis. Although each letter will be different, all may be considered examples of good writing, depending on what each writer wants to convey.

The audience member who was not personally acquainted with the speaker might write this:

Dear Ms. Gastone:

I thoroughly enjoyed your talk at the convention in Sacramento on March 24. I was especially interested in the new series of exercise videos that your company will be releasing next spring.

Would you please send me complete details? I am looking for new materials for our health and fitness club, and I am hoping your videos will be just the resource we need.

Thank you again for such an inspirational speech.

Cordially,

That's a good letter—friendly, but to the point. However, what if the speaker turned out to be an old friend? Perhaps another audience member was indeed a friend, but there was no chance to talk after the speech. The friend might write this:

Dear Carla:

It was a great surprise seeing you at the convention in Sacramento. I thought your talk was superb, and the rest of the audience was obviously equally impressed.

As training director here at Halliburton Fitness, I'm always on the lookout for the latest trends in wellness and sports fitness, and I was intrigued by the discussion of your company's exercise videos. I'd really appreciate any information you can send now, even though the release date is this fall.

I'm sorry we didn't have a chance to visit, but you were mobbed after your speech, and I had to catch a plane. Next time, let's plan some time together—we've got a lot of catching up to do. Did you know that Billy Richards is now the managing director of the Singapore Hilton?

Take care,

Both of these letters are good. Both writers asked for information to help their employers, and both writers were courteous to the speaker. Even though only the second was a personal friend, both letters were friendly, and both writers presented themselves as potential customers. In short, each of these letters will get the response that was hoped for—professional information and the renewal of an old friendship.

Promote Goodwill in Your Communications

Perhaps you enjoy shopping at a favorite store. You might prefer this store because it is more conveniently located than other stores, or the prices appeal to you, or the people who wait on you are cheerful and courteous. The owners want you to think of them when you need merchandise or services.

Goodwill is that feeling of confidence that makes a customer buy from one firm rather than another. Although goodwill is an intangible asset, it can very much affect the worth of a business. A firm's reputation is enhanced by:

- Turning out products or services that appeal to customers
- Selling at reasonable prices
- Dealing fairly with employees, customers, and suppliers
- Supporting local community activities
- Donating money or services to worthy causes

If a company has a reputation for shoddy products, unfair prices, and a condescending attitude toward people, then the goodwill is negative. Business owners and executives know that a poor public image will eventually be translated into poor sales and low profits. Without friends and supporters—without goodwill—the business will eventually perish.

Building goodwill—and holding it—is an important requirement of business writing. Typical goodwill letters are those that say *thank you, we appreciate, we congratulate, we're sorry about our error,* and so on. Many of the people you write never enter your place of business, never see you, and rarely talk to you. Their impressions of your business and their attitudes toward it are formed entirely through the letters and other written communications they receive.

Business communications—including e-mails, letters, sales materials, and more—certainly can contribute to a firm's positive public image and favorable public relations. A business correspondence, therefore, is more than a representative—it is also an ambassador. Business writers must be sensitive to others' needs and feelings if their writing is to be effective. Communications that are friendly, helpful, courteous, and tactful build goodwill.

The Audiences for Goodwill Letters

There are four different audiences for goodwill letters: employees, customers, the public, and suppliers.

Employees

When a manager compliments an employee in writing for outstanding achievement, it helps to build good employee relations. A written message is often much more effective than a spoken one. In turn, satisfied employees do their best in dealing with customers and clients.

Dear Jan:

Your presentation to the electronics group was most impressive. Your expertise in connector specifications assures them that our applications are on the mark. I noticed that Mark O'Brien was taking notes. Now that's a first!

Nice job. I'm glad you're on our team.

Best,

Customers

Good relations with customers are essential. These are the people who keep the company in business, and we go out of our way to keep them happy. Many firms offer special incentives to reward loyalty and attract new customers.

Dear Ms. Harrison:

You already know how convenient it is to have Ferguson Springs Bottled Water delivered right to your front door. With your next delivery, you'll receive a free one-liter sports size bottle of water. It's a perfect carry-along size for people on the go. It's our way of thanking you for being a good customer.

Tell your friends about us. For every friend that signs up for home delivery, we'll give you one month free. Just tell them to mention your name, and we'll take care of the rest.

Sincerely,

The Public

Typically, most company employees live in or near the town where the company is located. A business can enhance its reputation when it maintains good public relations within the local community.

Dear Dr. Orsini:

I was in the audience when you spoke to the Commonwealth Club last evening, and I wanted you to know how much I enjoyed your talk.

The Commonwealth Club has been doing a wonderful job leading the drive to construct and maintain a Senior Citizens Recreation Center here in town. Your leadership has been an inspiration to us all. I'm looking forward to attending the ribbon-cutting ceremonies next month.

Cordially,

Suppliers

Many companies, such as those in manufacturing or certain service industries, rely heavily on outside suppliers. Executives and owners of these companies are well aware of how important it is to have a good relationship with their vendors and subcontractors.

Dear Bob:

Thanks again for making sure that our heavy equipment was transported to the north side of the city yesterday. Because you managed to get it on the construction site before 6 a.m.—in spite of road construction, village ordinances, overtime, and flat tires—we were able to complete our part of the job right on schedule, thus avoiding a huge penalty.

You went the extra mile for us on this one, and I want you to know that we are most grateful.

Sincerely,

Use Concise Language

If you're one of those writers who need 100 words to say what might have been said in 40, you need to tighten up your prose. The wasted words we're talking about here are those that clutter the page and detract from your message without adding anything to it. If you want to write effective business communications, start editing your writing to eliminate nonsense words and phrases, repetition, and redundancies.

Here's an example of verbose writing that can be greatly improved by taking out the excess words and phrases.

Original (50 words) With reference to your request for an extension on your note under the date of March 20, we have considered the matter carefully and are pleased to be able to tell you that we will be willing to allow you an additional 90 days to make payment on your note.

Edited (18 words) We can allow you an additional 90 days to pay your note. It is now due June 20.

There was no sacrifice in meaning by eliminating the excess words. Indeed, the shortened message is clearer and, therefore, stronger.

Here is another example of writing that is cluttered with extra words and phrases. The edited version has a more conversational and friendlier tone. Although this is a covering letter, it offers the opportunity for the writer to build goodwill.

Original (61 words) With reference to your recent request on June 26 for 20 reprints of "How Good Are Sales Aptitude Tests?" in the May issue of *Modern Marketing Management*, these copies are enclosed for your convenience.

With appreciation for your kind remarks about this article and trusting you will find it very useful in your recruitment seminar in October, I remain,

Yours truly,

Edited (29 words) Enclosed are your 20 reprints of "How Good Are Sales Aptitude Tests?" I'm pleased you liked the article and hope it will be useful in your recruitment seminar.

Cordially,

In this example, the writer is adding a lot of extra information that is not particularly relevant. The writer points out an apparent contradiction that is of some interest, but discussing it gets in the way of what the writer really wants to know.

Original (64 words) In looking over your current catalog, I notice that the sofa on page 50 (No. 273-1960) is shown in the illustration in the color of blue. However, in the description provided under the illustration, the colors listed as being available are black, ivory, green, and red. Does this mean that the color of the couch in the illustration is not available at this time?

Edited (7 words) Is sofa (No. 273-1960) available in blue?

Here's a list of wordy phrases that are used too often in business writing. Compare the original phrase with the edited phrase.

Original	Edited
A large segment of the business management population is of the opinion that	Many executives believe that
At all times	Always
At an early date	Soon *or give date*
At that time	Then
At this point in time	At this time

Original	_Edited_
Due to the fact that	Because _or_ Since
During the course of	During
During the course of our research, we learned	Our research shows
Engaged in making a marketing study	Making a marketing study
He made the announcement that	He announced that
Held a meeting to discuss	Met to discuss
I hope that you will be in a position to make a decision within a short time.	I hope you can decide soon.
In the event that	If
Inasmuch as	Since
It is the recommendation of the committee that	The committee recommends that
Keep in mind the fact that	Remember that
The costs were quite a bit lower than any of us thought they would be.	The costs were lower than expected.
The difficulty with the present system is that it cannot be depended on.	The present system is not dependable.
The size of the report is 112 pages in length	The report is 112 pages _or_ The 112-page report
There was only one objection to your proposal, and that was the matter of timing.	The only objection to your proposal was timing.

Original	Edited
These items are being sold at a price of $5.	These items are priced at $5.
Until such time as you are in a position to	When you can *or* When you are able to
Upon completion, please mail the application in the envelope that is being enclosed.	Please return the completed application in the enclosed envelope.
Your check in the amount of $200	Your check for $200

Say It Once

A common fault of some letter writers is repetition. They use the same words (or a form of those words) and phrases repeatedly in the same paragraph. In the following examples, the repetitive words or phrases are in italics.

Repetitive	Edited
Although it is our policy to *accept returned merchandise* that is in good condition, *returned merchandise* that is not salable cannot be *accepted.*	We accept for returns only merchandise that can be resold.
It is *possible* that the damage occurred because of faulty packing. An even greater *possibility* is that the *shipper* was careless in storing the merchandise for safe *shipment.* In any event, we'll do everything *possible* to *ship* a replacement this week.	The damage may have been caused by faulty packing, or more likely, improper storage by the shipper. In any event, we'll try to send a replacement this week.
Most industrial relations specialists recommend that *employees participate* in job evaluation, although many employers think that *employee participation* is not desirable.	Most industrial relations specialists recommend that employees participate in job evaluation, although employers do not always share this point of view.

Repetitive

When we print your *form letters,* your customers will not recognize them as *form letters.* The *letters* will appear to be individually typewritten.

Edited

Your printed form letters will look individually typewritten.

Another form of repetition is redundancy. This is when expressions are superfluous, or unnecessary, and contain repetitive words. For example, *revert back* means *revert.* A *complete monopoly* is simply a *monopoly.* Here are more examples:

Redundant	Edited
Agree and concur	Agree *or* Concur
And etc. *or* et cetera and so forth	Etc. *or* Et cetera
Assemble together	Assemble
Baffling and puzzling	Baffling *or* Puzzling
Both alike	Alike
Consensus of opinion	Consensus
Contractual agreement	Contract *or* Agreement
Cooperate together	Cooperate
Customary practice	Custom *or* Practice
Depreciate in value	Depreciate
Endorse on the back of the check	Endorse the check
Final completion	Completion
First and foremost	First *or* Foremost
Fiscal financial year	Fiscal year

Redundant	Edited
Free gratis	Free *or* Gratis
In the near future	Soon *or give date*
Invisible to the eye	Invisible
Lose out	Lose
Massively large	Massive *or* Large
Monday morning at 10 o'clock a.m.	Monday morning at ten *or* Monday at 10 a.m.
New beginner	Beginner
Past experience	Experience
Prompt and speedy	Prompt *or* Speedy
Rarely ever	Rarely
Refer back to	Refer to
Repeat again	Repeat
The only other alternative	The only alternative
True facts	Facts
Vitally essential	Vital *or* Essential

Sentence Length

The length and structure of your sentences are important factors in making your letters easy and interesting to read. Readers lose track of the meaning in long, rambling sentences.

Because of our limited warehouse facilities, we are studying the possibility of contracting with public warehouses and handling facilities, charging their customers only for the space occupied and the length of time it is used.

By breaking one long sentence into several short ones, the message is simplified and made more understandable.

Because of our limited warehouse facilities, we are studying the possibility of using public warehouses. Several in this area offer storage and handling services. Most charge only for the space occupied and the length of time it is used.

Paragraph Length

Try to avoid long, fat paragraphs that give readers no visual breather. Solid blocks of type are hurdles for readers, and writers should look for ways to break up these paragraphs.

Many employees simplify their planning by sorting incoming correspondence according to some particular method—for example, by subject matter. All letters that pertain to one topic are answered before moving on to another topic. These employees say that separating the correspondence by subject matter improves their concentration. Others prefer to sort their correspondence according to difficulty. Some take the easy ones first, others the tougher ones. There seems to be no hard-and-fast rule about this. And a third method of sorting mail is according to urgency—the most pressing items first, regardless of subject matter or level of difficulty, and employees who are frequently interrupted maintain that this type of sorting is a must.

Difficult reading? Yes. To make it readable, break it down into several short paragraphs. Even better, add headings to make the content clear at a glance.

Most employees simplify their planning by sorting correspondence according to three yardsticks—subject matter, difficulty, and urgency.

Subject Matter

All letters that pertain to one topic are answered before moving on to another topic. Those who use this plan say it improves their concentration.

Difficulty

Other employees prefer to sort their correspondence according to difficulty. Some take the easy ones first, others the tougher ones.

A third method of sorting mail is according to urgency, with the most pressing items first, regardless of subject matter or level of difficulty. Employees who are frequently interrupted maintain that this type of sorting is a must.

Letter Length

For most correspondence, it's best to keep the letter to one page in length. If the letter requires additional pages, be sure to use a heading. For example, include the name of the addressee, page number, and date at the top of each page:

Jane P. Johnson
Page 2
January 1, 2006

Keep Language Simple

Some letter writers have the notion that big words are always best. Yet no matter how many communication experts warn against abstruse expressions, there are always those who continue to write using stuffy, overblown language.

We do not discount the importance of a rich vocabulary and "big words." Indeed, in many instances, there are no satisfactory substitutes. As long as you use the word correctly and are certain that your readers or listeners are not baffled by it, go right ahead. The occasional polysyllable can add spice to your writing.

For most correspondence, however, choose the word that you know is familiar to most people. Nearly everybody responds more warmly to the word *home* than to *domicile.* In a crowded movie theater there will be no rush to the exits if someone yells, *"Conflagration!"* But watch them make tracks when they hear, *"Fire!"*

There is an often-told tale about P. T. Barnum, who had a hard time getting crowds to leave his circus sideshows once they paid to get in. To make room for other customers waiting in line, he posted the sign, THIS WAY TO THE EGRESS. Thinking this was another exciting attraction, visitors followed the sign, only to find themselves outside the tent. *Egress,* of course, is a fancy word for *exit.*

When writing a letter, express yourself pretty much as you would if you were facing your reader. Would you write the following to your supervisor?

My analytical evaluation of the incentive plan that has been instituted revealed myriad discrepancies and inconsistencies with the inevitable result that serious inequities prevail among personnel.

Of course you wouldn't. Here is probably what you would write:

I've studied our present incentive plan carefully, and I think some changes are in order. What bothers me most is that the plan is very fair to some, but not at all fair to others.

It's always a good idea to choose the simple word over the formal, or showy, word. The reason is that conversational writing is livelier and more interesting. Here is a list of formal words and their conversational equivalents.

Formal	*Conversational*
Cogitate upon	Think about
Be cognizant of	Know that
Comprehend	See *or* Understand
Comprised	Made up of
Conjecture	Think *or* Believe
Consummate	Finish *or* Agree to
Corroborate	Confirm *or* Make sure
Deliberate upon	Think about
Disbursements	Payments
Increment	Increase *or* Raise
Maximal	Fullest
Initial	First
Nominal	Small *or* Little

Formal	Conversational
Obviate	Make unnecessary
Origination	Beginning
Proclivity	Leaning *or* Tendency
Predicated	Based
Ratify	Approve *or* Confirm
Rationale	Basis *or* Reason
Remunerate	Pay
Scrutinize	Read *or* Examine *or* Inspect *or* Look at
Transpire	Happen *or* Take place
Ultimate	Final

Here are some examples of formal writing. Compare the stiff, puffed-up style to the more informal conversational style:

Formal	Conversational
The contract enclosed herewith requires your signature before it can be executed and should be directed to the undersigned.	Please sign the enclosed contract and return it to me.
Due to a low inventory situation, we are reluctantly compelled to transmit a partial shipment of 5 Crescent motors in lieu of the 12 that were requested. We anticipate shipment of the remainder subsequent.	I'm sending five Crescent motors today. The remaining seven will go out to you just as soon as we get a new shipment— probably next week.
The expeditious manner in which you executed our high-priority order for maple seedlings is hereby gratefully acknowledged.	The maple seedlings arrived this morning, and I thank you for your fast service.

Formal	Conversational
Commensurate with standard practice in the industry, as a wholesale enterprise our organization must decline direct distribution to consumers. Undoubtedly you can satisfy your requirements at a local retail establishment in the Atlanta area.	As wholesalers, we sell only to retail outlets. Several stores in Atlanta carry Oneida appliances. An up-to-date list is on our Web site.
Your recalcitrance in expediting payment of your obligations obviates consideration of further extension of credit privileges, and we foresee no viable alternative than cancellation of aforesaid privileges.	Because you continually make late payments on your outstanding loan, we are not able to offer you additional credit.

Overused Words

Business writing is full of overused words, many ending in *-ize*. More and more often we see and hear words like *legitimize, politicize, factionalize, strategize, accessorize, finalize, maximize,* and so on. Although these words are generally found in a dictionary, they are so overused as to make written communications seem trite.

For example, the word *prioritize* appears often, as in:

The matter of cost control must be prioritized.

Avoid this overused word by simply stating:

Make cost control a priority.

There is also a growing tendency to tack on the suffix *-wise*. We're bombarded with overused words like *policywise, procedurewise, weightwise, saleswise, sizewise,* and more. Like *-ize* words, these too are overused.

The suffix *-uate,* tacked onto certain words to indicate action, is also overused, particularly by business writers. There are many good *-uate* words—such as *perpetuate, evaluate, fluctuate, and evacuate*—but *actuate, effectuate,* and *eventuate* are not among them. Here are some overused words, and suggestions for saying the same thing another way.

Overused Words	Restated
The plans are finalized.	The plans are complete.
We strategized.	We planned.
The sales team maximized their efforts.	The sales team put forth their best efforts.
This appears to be the right thing to do profitwise.	I think the new plan will result in bigger profits.
Costwise, it is inadvisable for sales representatives to concentrate on sparsely populated areas.	We can cut costs by working only those territories where we can expect volume sales.
Distancewise, it's a toss-up between Colfax and Denton as a new plant location.	Colfax and Denton are about the same distance away, so mileage is not a factor in choosing one over the other.
I can see no effect moralewise on personnel under this new policy.	I doubt that employee morale will be affected by this new policy.
We expect to actuate the revised retirement plan early next year.	The revised retirement plan goes into effect early next year.
It is our hope that the results of the study will eventuate in substantial savings.	We hope our study will result in substantial savings.

Trendy Words

Like clothing fads, terminology comes and goes. It seems that whenever a sophisticated sounding word is used once, the business bureaucrats immediately seize on it.

Today there are no alternatives except *viable* ones. People who have a personal appeal are *charismatic*. When people disagree on a particular issue, there is a *dichotomy*. When we struggle to make a decision, we *interface* with the problem. When we offer an opinion, we take a *posture* or *stance*. When our points of view are different, there is *polarization*. The list of vogue words is endless.

A recent verbal fad is the tendency to use nouns as verbs, as in:

How will the move impact employee turnover?

Better to restate the question as:

What impact will the move have on employee turnover?

If you feel that there's nothing wrong with these overused words, that's up to you. We urge you, however, to use plain English in your letters. It is the simple word, the natural word, the conversational word, the everyday word that will do the most to make your writing readable, interesting, and persuasive.

Personalize Your Letters

Letters are written by one person and sent to one or more others. Even though you use a company letterhead and represent an organization when you write, it's still you who delivers the message. If you are allowed to write as you please, remember to treat your readers well. Most of your business associates are reasonable, civilized, thoughtful, and friendly, and they like to be treated as though they're important.

Dear Sir:

This will acknowledge your order for 16 Multi-Craft belt sanders and 8 disc grinders. This order will be shipped promptly. Thank you for your business.

Yours truly,

This letter is certainly acceptable. The writer said what was necessary—order acknowledged, shipment will go forth promptly, and thank you. What was missing was a personal touch. Here is the same letter written by the sales representative who calls on this customer:

Dear Mr. Rosetti:

Thank you very much for your order of June 21.

I'm pleased that a reputable store like yours has decided to carry our Multi-Craft belt sanders. Based on past experience, I'm predicting that you'll have such success with our sanders that you'll soon want to carry our complete line of tools for the home craftsman.

If I can be of any help with your display and promotion, let me know. Other-wise, I'll see you the week of July 12.

Best regards,

The second letter should leave no doubt in Mr. Rosetti's mind that he is a special new customer. Some writers like to personalize their letters by using the recipient's name in the body of the letter. This technique is fine, but be careful not to overdo it.

If I can be of any help with your display and promotion, Mr. Rosetti, let me know.

The following letter was written by a town tax supervisor to a property owner who pointed out that she had paid her property tax twice.

Madam:

The enclosed check for $378.88 is due you because of the duplicate payment of taxes on your property.

Yours truly,

The above letter will not make the taxpayer cranky. She wanted a refund and she got it. But rather than treat her as just another anonymous taxpayer, it would be just as easy to write this letter as follows:

Dear Ms. Guilford:

You're right—there was a duplicate payment of your property taxes, and the enclosed check for $378.88 is your refund.

Our audit procedures would have eventually discovered the error, but you speeded things up by calling the matter to our attention. Thanks for your help.

Sincerely,

Form Letters

Many people are unable to exert the effort in answering routine letters that they put into personalized letters. You might consider preparing a model letter for each frequently recurring situation, then adapting it to fit the circumstances. Here's an example.

Dear _____:

Thank you for your interest in working for Hutchinson-McGee Corporation.

At the present time, we have no job openings, and we cannot predict when there will be one. However, we will keep your application on file for six months and contact you if an opening occurs that matches your qualifications.

Sincerely,

Using Personal Pronouns

Many of us were taught that it was best to avoid using the pronoun *I* in business letters, and wherever possible, to use the pronoun *you*. In today's business world either is acceptable.

Using *I* makes your letters personal, and you should use it as naturally as if you were carrying on a conversation with a friend.

I'm delighted to learn about your promotion to product manager.

You is also a good word that should show up frequently in your letters, but if you overdo it, you can sound patronizing.

You are to be congratulated on your promotion to product manager.

The point is, you needn't struggle for ways to use *you* and avoid *I*. Use both pronouns, along with *your, me, and my,* when it seems natural to do so.

It is sometimes difficult to choose between *I* and *we* in letters concerning business matters. In most cases, the choice is up to the writer. Depending on the situation, you should feel free to use either pronoun.

Use *I* when you want your letter to have a personal from-me-to-you feel.

I very much enjoyed your visit to my office last Tuesday. Enclosed are the materials I promised to send you.

We is preferable when the writer speaks for the company and not just for himself or herself.

Thank you for calling this situation to our attention, Mr. Culver. We appreciate your patience with us.

Emphasize the Positive

Most of the letters you write will have some sales content. You don't have to be selling a product. Only a relatively small percentage of business letters are written for this specific purpose. But if you're an effective writer, you try to make or keep friends and customers, persuade readers to accept an idea (whether it's an apology or a proposal), or build a favorable image for your company. Call it what you will—tact, warmth, friendliness, enthusiasm—any method you use to persuade people to think well of you is still salesmanship.

You can emphasize the positive in your letters in several ways:

- Stress what you can do, not what you can't.
- Avoid negative words and phrases.
- Respond promptly.

Stress What You Can Do

If you cannot satisfy a customer's request, offer an alternate solution. For example, a mail order firm advertises purses for $44.95 in brown, tan, and black leather. The black purses quickly sold out, but a new shipment is expected within 10 days. Here is a negative response to a customer who ordered a black purse.

Dear Ms. Dillon:

I'm sorry that we are currently out of stock of black leather purses. We will be unable to fill your order at this time.

An order has been placed with the manufacturer for the color you want, but it will be at least 10 days before we will receive shipment. I trust this delay will not inconvenience you.

Sincerely,

The above letter contains a number of negative words and phrases: *I'm sorry, unable, delay, inconvenience.* Now compare it to the following positive response.

Dear Ms. Dillon:

Thank you for ordering a black leather purse.

The color you chose proved to be very popular, and we quickly sold all we had in stock. However, we've placed a rush order for more and are promised delivery within 10 days. Yours will be shipped the same day our new supply arrives.

We appreciate your patience, and we know you'll be delighted with this beautifully designed purse. It's very handsome, and like our other leather products, it is also very rugged.

Cordially,

Avoid Negative Words and Phrases

Be especially careful in your letters not to use words describing people, intentions, or actions that will be offensive. Compare the following examples of negative and positive statements.

Negative	Positive
You neglected to specify the color of vinyl sheeting you require.	Let me know the color of vinyl sheeting you prefer.
Your complaint is regrettable.	I'm sorry that our product did not live up to your expectations.
You claim that you did not understand our discount terms.	The terms of sale are described on our invoice, and perhaps you overlooked them.

Negative	Positive
Frankly, I am surprised at your insinuation.	Let me explain how this problem came about.
Your alibi for skipping the March payment on your promissory note is lame.	Thank you for explaining why you did not make payment in March on your promissory note.
I dispute your assertion that the merchandise we sent was inferior.	I think you'll agree that the shirts you received matched the specifications on page 321 of our catalog.
Surely you don't expect us to violate company policy by extending six-month credit terms to you.	We allowed you four months to pay for your October order. This is the maximum time permitted under our standard policy.
You should know by now that we need at least two weeks' lead time in filling orders for imported articles.	As indicated in our catalog, we need at least two weeks lead time in filling orders for imported articles.
You obviously ignored the assembly instructions accompanying the equipment.	The assembly instructions accompanying the equipment are very specific. I'm enclosing another set in case you misplaced those in the original package.
You failed to enclose your check. Obviously we can't credit your account until we receive payment.	You have probably already discovered that the check you meant to enclose was missing. If you have not already mailed it, please do so at your earliest convenience.

Respond Promptly

Promptness in attending to your correspondence nearly always reveals a positive attitude. It shows you're eager to be of service, you respect your correspondents' time, and you want them to be impressed by your efficiency. Customers may take their business elsewhere when company representatives are too slow in answering their mail.

When you receive a letter to which you cannot respond fully, acknowledge it immediately and say when you will have the needed information or decision.

Thanks for sending the sample cartons. Two of my colleagues who must see the samples before a final decision can be reached are out of town until November 14. I expect we can reach a decision within a day or two of their return, and you'll hear from me then.

But Not Necessarily Too Promptly

There are times when promptness in answering letters may not be wise, even though you are prepared to make a full response immediately. For example, you may have received a proposal or an offer and you know the answer is no.

If you respond too quickly, the recipient of your letter might feel that you gave their idea little thought because your mind was closed from the start. Replying too promptly is also a bad idea when dealing with longtime clients who ask for special favors that you're not in a position to grant. They want to feel that you at least gave their request due consideration.

When you have to say no to people who offer what you can't use or who ask a favor you can't grant, it may be best to let your correspondence age a bit before responding. You could write a quick note acknowledging their offer, and then, after an appropriate interval, politely decline their suggestion.

Thanks for your proposal regarding Brinkmeyer Accounting Systems. This matter deserves careful study, and I will be in touch with you about it later.

Be sure to take all the time you need when writing long reports or addressing matters of extra importance or great sensitivity. It's a good idea to prepare a rough draft and put it aside for a few hours or days. Reread it from time to time to make sure you have written exactly what is appropriate under the circumstances.

Part 2

CHOOSE THE BEST FORMAT

First impressions count, so take care to present your correspondence using the most appropriate format.

Letters have long been the most common form of business correspondence. Letters are formal, traditional, and present your company in a positive light. Letters are especially appropriate when you are writing to new and prospective customers.

Memos also have a long tradition in business. They are typically written to fellow coworkers within the company. The format and tone is less formal than a business letter.

E-mails have replaced letters and memos for the most part, especially when it comes to routine business matters. E-mails are typically informal in tone, short, and suggest that an immediate response is needed. Most businesses have an in-house computer network where employees can contact one another via e-mail or IM (Instant Message). Employees can also use the Internet to send e-mails to customers and clients. E-mails are good to use when you have an established relationship with your client.

Faxes are useful for saving time when transmitting documents. In some cases a hard copy will be mailed after the document is faxed.

Voice mail is the most informal means of communicating, but this method should be treated with respect. If you are leaving a voice mail message, be sure to include all pertinent information, including where you can be reached for a return phone call.

Letters

Readers get their first impression of a business letter even before they read it. The quality of paper, letterhead design, placement of the message on the page, and letter style all have something to say about an organization. A weakness in any of these elements can detract from the effectiveness of the message, even though it is expertly written.

Letter Style

There are several letter styles, or layouts, to choose from. A few companies select a style and insist that everyone use it, but in most cases the choice is up to the writer. The three most popular styles are semiblocked, blocked, and full blocked.

Semiblocked Style

In the semiblocked style, the dateline starts at the middle of the page, as does the complimentary close. Each paragraph is indented five spaces.

Date

Name
Title
Company Name
Street
City, State, Zip

Dear Name:

     This is the beginning of paragraph one. Xxxxxxxxxxxxxxxxxxx. Xxxxxxxxxxxxxxxxxxxxxxxxxxxxxxxxxxxxxxxxxxxxxxxxxxxxxxxxxxxx. Xxxxxxxxxxxxxxxxxxxxxxxxxxxxxxxxxxxxxxxxxxxxxxxxxxxxxxxxxxxxx xxxxxxxxxxxxxxxxxxxxxxxxxxxxxxxxxxxxxxxxxxxxxxxxxxxxxxxxxxxxx xxxxxxxxxxxxxxxxxxxxxxxxxxxxxxxxxxxxxxxxxxxxxx.

     This is the beginning of paragraph two. Xxxxxxxxxxxxx. xxxxxx. Xxxxxxxxxxxxxxxxxxxxxxxxxxxxxxxxxxxxxxxxxxxxxxxxxxxxxxxxxxxxx xxxxxxxxxxxxxxxxxxxxxxxxxxxxxxxxxxxxxxxxxxxxxxxxxxxxxxxxxxxxx xxxxxxxxxxxxxxxxxxxxxxxxxxxxxxxxxxxxxxxxxxxxxxxxxxxxxxxxxxxxx xxxxxxxxxxxxxxxxxxxxxxxxxxxxxxxxxxxxxxxxxxxxxxxxxxxxxxxxxxxxx xxxxxxxxxxxxxxxxxxxxxxxxxxxxxxxxxxxxxxxxxxxxxxxxxxxxxxxxxxxxx Xxxxxxxxxxxxxxxxxxxxxxxxxxxxxxxxxxxxxxxxxxxxxxxxxxxxxxxxxxxxx xxxxxxxxx.

     This is the beginning of paragraph three. Xxxxxxxxxxxxxxxx. Xxxxxxxxxxxxxxxxxxxxxxxxxxxxxxxxxxxxxxxxxxxxxxxxxxxxxxxxxxxxx xxxxxxxxxxxxxxxxxxxxxxxxxxxxxxxxxxxxxxxxxxxxxxxxxxxxxxxxxxxxx xxxxxxxxxxxxxxxxxxxxxxxxxxxxxxxxxxxxxxxxxxxxxxxxxxxxxxxxxxxxx xxxxxxxxxxxxxxxxxxxxx.

Complimentary close,

Writer
Title

Blocked Style   The only change in this style from the semiblocked one is that the paragraphs are not indented.

```
                                                          Date

           Name
           Title
           Company Name
           Street
           City, State, Zip

           Dear Name:

           This is the beginning of paragraph one. Xxxxxxxxxxxxxxxxxxxxxxxx.
           Xxxxxxxxxxxxxxxxxxxxxxxxxxxxxxxxxxxxxxxxxxxxxxxxxxxxxxxxxxxxxx.
           Xxxxxxxxxxxxxxxxxxxxxxxxxxxxxxxxxxxxxxxxxxxxxxxxxxxxxxxxxxxxxx
           xxxxxxxxxxxxxxxxxxxxxxxxxxxxxxxxxxxxxxxxxxxxxxxxxxxxxxxxxxxxxx
           xxxxxxxxxxxxxxxxxxxxxxxxxxxxxxxxxxxxxxxxxxxxxxx.

           This is the beginning of paragraph two. Xxxxxxxxxxxxxxxxx. xxxxxx.
           Xxxxxxxxxxxxxxxxxxxxxxxxxxxxxxxxxxxxxxxxxxxxxxxxxxxxxxxxxxxxxx
           xxxxxxxxxxxxxxxxxxxxxxxxxxxxxxxxxxxxxxxxxxxxxxxxxxxxxxxxxxxxxx
           xxxxxxxxxxxxxxxxxxxxxxxxxxxxxxxxxxxxxxxxxxxxxxxxxxxxxxxxxxxxxx
           xxxxxxxxxxxxxxxxxxxxxxxxxxxxxxxxxxxxxxxxxxxxxxxxxxxxxxxxxxxxxx
           xxxxxxxxxxxxxxxxxxxxxxxxxxxxxxxxxxxxxxxxxxxxxxxxxxxxxxxxxxxxxx
           Xxxxxxxxxxxxxxxxxxxxxxxxxxxxxxxxxxxxxxxxxxxxxxxxxxxxxxxxxxxxxx
           xxxxxxxxx.

           This is the beginning of paragraph three. Xxxxxxxxxxxxxxxxxxxxxxxx.
           Xxxxxxxxxxxxxxxxxxxxxxxxxxxxxxxxxxxxxxxxxxxxxxxxxxxxxxxxxxxxxx
           xxxxxxxxxxxxxxxxxxxxxxxxxxxxxxxxxxxxxxxxxxxxxxxxxxxxxxxxxxxxxx
           xxxxxxxxxxxxxxxxxxxxxxxxxxxxxxxxxxxxxxxxxxxxxxxxxxxxxxxxxxxxxx
           xxxxxxxxxxxxxxxxxxxx.

                                               Complimentary close,

                                               Writer
                                               Title
```

Full Blocked Style

Here, every element is placed flush with the left margin.

Date

Name
Title
Company Name
Street
City, State, Zip

Dear Name:

This is the beginning of paragraph one. Xxxxxxxxxxxxxxxxxxxxxxxxxx.
Xxxxxxxxxxxxxxxxxxxxxxxxxxxxxxxxxxxxxxxxxxxxxxxxxxxxxxxxxxxxxxxx.
Xxxxxxxxxxxxxxxxxxxxxxxxxxxxxxxxxxxxxxxxxxxxxxxxxxxxxxxxxxxxxxxx
xxxxxxxxxxxxxxxxxxxxxxxxxxxxxxxxxxxxxxxxxxxxxxxxxxxxxxxxxxxxxxxx
xxxxxxxxxxxxxxxxxxxxxxxxxxxxxxxxxxxxxxxxxxxxxxxxxxxxx.

This is the beginning of paragraph two. Xxxxxxxxxxxxxxxxxx. xxxxxx.
Xxxxxxxxxxxxxxxxxxxxxxxxxxxxxxxxxxxxxxxxxxxxxxxxxxxxxxxxxxxxxxxx
xxxxxxxxxxxxxxxxxxxxxxxxxxxxxxxxxxxxxxxxxxxxxxxxxxxxxxxxxxxxxxxx
xxxxxxxxxxxxxxxxxxxxxxxxxxxxxxxxxxxxxxxxxxxxxxxxxxxxxxxxxxxxxxxx
xxxxxxxxxxxxxxxxxxxxxxxxxxxxxxxxxxxxxxxxxxxxxxxxxxxxxxxxxxxxxxxx
xxxxxxxxxxxxxxxxxxxxxxxxxxxxxxxxxxxxxxxxxxxxxxxxxxxxxxxxxxxxxxxx
Xxxxxxxxxxxxxxxxxxxxxxxxxxxxxxxxxxxxxxxxxxxxxxxxxxxxxxxxxxxxxxxx
xxxxxxxxx.

This is the beginning of paragraph three. Xxxxxxxxxxxxxxxxxxxxxxxxx.
Xxxxxxxxxxxxxxxxxxxxxxxxxxxxxxxxxxxxxxxxxxxxxxxxxxxxxxxxxxxxxxxx
xxxxxxxxxxxxxxxxxxxxxxxxxxxxxxxxxxxxxxxxxxxxxxxxxxxxxxxxxxxxxxxx
xxxxxxxxxxxxxxxxxxxxxxxxxxxxxxxxxxxxxxxxxxxxxxxxxxxxxxxxxxxxxxxx
xxxxxxxxxxxxxxxxxxxxx.

Complimentary close,

Writer
Title

Paper

Paper quality is based on weight and what is used to make the paper. Paper weight is determined by the manufacturer and often varies from one brand to the next. In many companies letterhead paper is a 20-pound weight with a 25 percent cotton-fiber (rag) content. In others, a 16-pound bond of the same rag content is standard. Some executives choose a 24-pound bond with 50 to 100 percent rag content for personal and social correspondence. If high quality is enormously important to the image of the firm, the company may choose this more expensive paper for all correspondence.

Bond paper comes in a wide variety of finishes—smooth, matte, ripple, and many others. You can select one of the standard finishes available, or you can have paper made with your own watermark. Envelopes and second sheets should always match the letterhead in quality and finish.

The least expensive stationery is made from recycled paper and sulfite. A 16-pound or 20-pound weight is commonly used for mass mailings, routine announcements, photocopies, and the like.

White is by far the most widely used color of stationery, but light tints—gray, blue, antique ivory, green, and other pastels—are also popular. Companies choose the color that they feel will be most attractive to their clientele and that best represents their product or service. For example, a legal firm might choose a somber gray tone, while a manufacturer of cosmetics may prefer to use a soft pink.

The standard size of letterhead paper is 8½ × 11 inches. For personal and social use, some managers and executives often choose a smaller size such as Monarch (7¼ × 10½ inches) or Baronial (5½ × 8½ inches). Envelopes should be chosen expressly for the size of letterhead used. The envelope ordinarily used for the standard letterhead is 4⅛ × 9½ inches and is referred to as a No. 10.

Margins, Spacing, and Placement

There should be at least a one-inch margin on either side of the letter. If the letter is short, you can increase your side margins to two inches or more.

The margins at the top and bottom edges of the paper are usually 1 to 1½ inches. When using letterhead, of course, the top margin will be established for you. Start approximately one inch below the logo.

Most business letters are single-spaced with one blank line between paragraphs. There is also a blank line between the inside address and the salutation, and between the salutation and the first line of the message. The complimentary close is one or two spaces below the last line of the letter. Allow three or four spaces for the signature.

Salutation

When writing to individuals, always use their names and titles, if appropriate. When writing to a personal friend or close business associate, use the first name. Address letters to female associates as *Ms.* instead of *Miss* or *Mrs.*

Dear Andy:

Dear Marla:

Dear Ms. Farlowe:

Dear Dr. Breedlove:

Dear Professor Quinlan:

If you are addressing an individual whose name you do not know—the purchasing manager, director of human resources, president, and so on—simply call the company and ask for the name.

Mr. John Samuelson
Director of Human Resources
Leverett Products Corporation
112 N. W. Lovejob
Portland, OR 97209

Dear Mr. Samuelson:

Attention or Subject Line

An attention line is occasionally placed between the address and salutation. This optional line is useful when directing your letter to the attention of a specific person or when it is important to draw attention to the subject matter.

Plymouth Rock Mfg. Co.
123 Atlantic Avenue
Boston, Massachusetts 02110

Attn: J. P. Scovill, Chief Engineer

Dear Sirs:

It is sometimes wise to indicate the subject of the letter.

Olivia Moreno, Claims Supervisor
Pacific Marine Insurance Company
254 Powell Street
San Francisco, California 94108

Re: Claim No. MAHR 457972

Dear Ms. Moreno:

Complimentary Close

A complimentary close is nearly always used in business letters. The wording you choose depends on you. Here are several personal closings:

Sincerely,

Sincerely yours,

Cordially,

Best wishes,

Warmest regards,

For a more formal closing, use one of these:

Yours truly,

Very truly yours,

E-mail

E-mail, or electronic mail, is the primary mode of written communication in today's business world. The benefits are many. Information can be passed along quickly: Ask a question via e-mail and you're likely to receive an immediate answer. E-mails are casual in language and format. E-mail is easy to manage—move it to an electronic file, save it in auxiliary memory, or delete it altogether. Most e-mail is left on the computer, but if necessary, you can print a hard copy.

The number of e-mails you receive can also be overwhelming. Depending on your job, you may receive 100 e-mail messages each day. You have to read each one quickly, then decide what to do with it. Some will contain useful information, others may require a response, and still others can probably be deleted once they are read. The messages you keep should be filed electronically to minimize clutter in your e-mail in box.

E-mail headings vary from one software program to the next, but typically you enter information at TO: [the addressee(s)], CC: [person(s) getting a copy], BCC: [person(s) getting a copy, name suppressed to addressee], and SUBJECT [the topic]. Your name [the writer] and the date sent are added automatically by the software program.

Write Effective E-mails

E-mails are informal, both in language and format. They are often written quickly so that you can move on to the next task.

The software program determines the exact format, but all include spaces for the writer to enter the name of the addressee, the names of people getting copies, and the subject matter. The sender's name is added by the software and will appear on the recipient's copy.

A salutation is optional, as is a signature. Most software programs give you the option of adding a sign-off tag line, such as your name, address, and contact information. You may choose to omit a sign-off altogether or perhaps simply end with your initials.

TO: Moira Crenshaw

CC: Jason Downing; Erin McGurdy; Jack Parong

BCC:

SUBJECT: Fanning installation

The Fanning installation was done by Jason's team, so we have documentation to show that all equipment was tested on site and the network was working properly. Now that the entire system has crashed, we need to put Erin on the case immediately. Fanning is saying the problem is our software, but my suspicion is that they brought in an outside "expert." If I'm right, then the contract is back in Jack's lap.

MC

Perhaps your workday begins like this: As soon as you arrive, you e-mail a coworker with an urgent question. While reading your e-mail, you respond to an irate customer's e-mail, offering assurance that the problem is being resolved. You receive an answer to your question a few minutes later, and now you can e-mail your supervisor with the status of an ongoing contract negotiation. Meanwhile, the phone is ringing, another coworker is waiting to talk to you, and the receptionist sends you an IM saying that a vendor has arrived per your scheduled appointment.

With a day like this one, your e-mails are going to be short and to the point. Here are some suggestions to make your e-mails more effective.

Deal with One Topic per E-mail

It's better to send one e-mail per subject than to combine everything in one longer e-mail. The idea is to make it easy for the addressee to respond, one subject at a time. When you combine subjects, one or more may be unintentionally ignored.

This e-mail is confusing because several subjects are addressed.

I need a job number for the OmniGlobe account. Also, who handles the Faire Lady Mall account? It used to be Kerry Baird's, but maybe it's been turned over to Jeff Cromwell by now. The new MacKenzie Motor Corp. catalog is being prepared. How many will we need for the Atlanta trade show? Let me know by the 4th.

By sending three separate e-mails, the addressee can quickly respond. No topic will be overlooked. And each e-mail can be saved, if desired, in the appropriate category.

What is the job number for the OmniGlobe account?

I need to update my records on Faire Lady Mall. Who is the sales person now handling this account?

The new MacKenzie Motor Corp. catalog is about to be printed. Last year we printed 2,500 for the Atlanta trade show. How many do you want this year? If there's a change, I'll need to know by Tuesday, the 4th.

Send Short Messages

It's best to limit the length of an e-mail message so it can be read in its entirety on one computer screen. You want your reader to get the information without having to reach for the computer mouse and scroll down to see the last few lines. It often helps to use bullet points or numbered lists to keep your message visually organized.

The information in this message is short, but at a glance it looks more complicated than it actually is.

It's important that our assessment of the Rockford plant go smoothly. Make sure you have enough copies of the presentation to hand out to all those in attendance. Are you going to be running 3 or 4 training sessions? We need to remind the Rockford group that attendance is required at one of them. One of the interns is making plane and hotel reservations for the three of us on the assessing team, but after last month's snafu, I'd appreciate it if you would follow up on that this week. Thanks.

Bullet points in this e-mail clarify what needs to be done.

In order to tie up any loose ends before we go to Rockford, I'd appreciate it if you would follow up on these issues:

- There should be a handout—a copy of the presentation—for each person attending. Bring extras.

- Remind the Rockford group that attendance is mandatory at your training session. Let them know when the sessions are scheduled so they can sign up in advance.

- Double-check on the plane and hotel reservations. We'd all like to avoid a repeat of last month's problems.

Thanks much.

Follow Normal Rules for Spelling, Punctuation, and Grammar

Many adults started using e-mail in high school and college. That was a good time and place to experiment with words and formatting. In the business world, however, it is important to return to standard rules for English language usage.

The message below is fine for a student, but inappropriate for business correspondence. Be sure to use appropriate spelling and punctuation. Omit your favorite cute symbols.

R U available for a con4ence 10 AM Fryday ? ⇒ **head honcho** will be there with bells on⧴ !!ding a ling!!   U R #5 on agenda. 👄⧴ look sharp 👄

The following message is hard to read, and the writer seems to be shouting. Use both upper- and lowercase letters.

MONTHLY MEETING FOR DEPARTMENT HEADS WILL BE 10 AM FRIDAY JUNE 22 ROOM 312. MARVIN SNYDER WILL BE CHAIRING THIS MONTH'S MEETING. AGENDA ATTACHED.

The next message is an appropriate business e-mail. The writer chooses a traditional font. Boldface and italic are used sparingly, and in this case, not at all.

The monthly meeting for department heads will be Friday, June 22, 10 a.m., room 312. Marvin Snyder will be chairing this month's meeting. An agenda is attached.

Use only those acronyms that are standard in business or your industry. Two commonly used business acronyms are FYI (For Your Information) and ASAP (As Soon As Possible). It's best to hide the fact that you are ROFL (Rolling On the Floor Laughing).

Be Conscious of E-mail Security Issues

E-mail is neither confidential nor secure. You cannot control if or to whom it will be forwarded. An unknown person can hack into your computer, then read and forward your e-mail without your knowledge. Many companies have the capability to check employee computers to verify that e-mails and Internet usage are appropriate and in keeping with company policy.

You are sitting in the privacy of your cubicle or office when you press Send. However, your e-mail isn't private—it's like sending a postcard. When an e-mail is intensely personal, full of anger or delightfully salacious, you can be sure that everyone will be reading it.

Before you send an e-mail ask yourself if you would be comfortable seeing your message in the newspaper or having it read aloud over your company's paging system. If that is okay, then it is okay to press Send. Otherwise, pick up the phone or walk to your coworker's cubicle and say what you have to say in person.

Memos

Memos are simply informal letters, and they are typically sent from one employee to another within the same company. The memo format has been largely replaced by e-mail, but memos do have their place, and they are still good choices when composing long messages and reports.

If your company no longer provides preprinted memo stationery, use company stationery and begin the memo with the following heading. It is similar to contemporary e-mail headings.

MEMO

To:

From:

Date:

Subject:

Body of memo xxxxxxxxxxxxxxxxxxxxxxxxxxxxxxxxxxxxxxxxxxxxxxxxxxxxxx xxxxxxxxxxxxxxxxxxxxxxxxxxxxxxxxxxxxxxxxxxxxxxxxxxxxxxxxxxxxxxxxxxxx xxxxxxxxxxxxxxxxxxxxxxxxxxxxxxxxxxxxxxxxxxxxxxxxxxxxxxxxxxxxxxxxxx xxxxxxxxxxxxxxxxxxxxxxxxxxxxxxxxxxxxxxxxxxxxxxxxxxxxxxxxxxxxxxxxxxx.

A salutation and complimentary close is optional. As in e-mails, most writers simply add their initials at the end of the message.

Faxes

Facsimile copies, or faxes, are digital pictures of documents. They are transmitted from one fax machine to another via telephone or cable lines. To send a fax, simply insert a document in your fax machine and dial the number of the receiving fax machine. Your fax machine will transmit a digitized picture of the document to the receiving machine.

Be aware that most faxes are digitized at a low resolution, so fine details rarely transmit well. If you are designing a form for users to fill in and fax to you, be sure to allow plenty of room for handwriting. The larger the handwriting, the easier it will be to read.

Faxes are often used for sending and receiving orders, contracts, and more. Faxes are particularly time-saving when it comes to signing contracts because faxed signatures are generally accepted as legally binding. In many instances a job cannot start until both parties sign a contract that spells out the details of the work to be done, the time frame in which it must be accomplished, and the price of parts and labor.

For example, in large construction projects, such as erecting an office high rise or repairing large sections of highway, the overseeing contractor uses a number of subcontractors. Each subcontractor must submit bids and sign contracts before the work can begin. Thanks to fax machines, the paperwork can be completed quickly—within the hour, if necessary. The overseeing company signs the contract, then faxes it to the subcontractor, who in turn signs and faxes it back. Now both firms have a signed contract on file and work can begin.

Fax Cover Sheet

It is likely that each fax machine in a company is shared by a number of employees. Therefore, it is important to prepare a cover sheet that identifies the recipient and the material being faxed. The cover sheet can be a separate sheet, or it can be a small tag on a corner of the first page.

In some cases it may be important to note that a specific piece of correspondence was sent as a fax. Simply add a notation to the top of the letter being sent.

Via Fax Transmission

Original sent via U.S. Mail

Fax Transmission/No hard copy to follow.

The message section is optional, but is often used to identify the content or remind the recipient that a response is required.

Here's the latest revision. Section III has been rewritten per Don's input.

Please sign on pages 6 and 7, and fax back those pages only.

Here is a sample cover sheet. There is plenty of room for the sender to fill in information by hand.

Sender's Letterhead

Name, Address, City, State, Zip

Phone Number, Fax Number

Fax Cover Sheet

Date: _____ No. of pages (incl. this one):_____

To:
_____
(Name)

_____
(Company)

_____
(Fax Number)

Message:

Take Advantage of Faxes

Fax machines are essential in the current business environment. Make sure that you're using your fax to its best advantage.

Make Your Fax Machine Available Day and Night

Connect your fax to its own phone line. Then leave it on all the time. One phone or cable line can be used for multiple calls, but too many users can slow down transmissions or interrupt them altogether. It's best to have one line dedicated to receiving and sending faxes. This is particularly important for businesses that communicate routinely via fax.

Fax machines do not require an operator to monitor them, so they can be turned on and left on. They are available to send and receive faxes regardless of the time zone.

Use a Cover Sheet

A cover sheet identifies the sender and recipient. It also includes the number of pages being faxed—a useful piece of information if several employees receive faxes from the same machine.

Be Conscious of Fax Security Issues

Be wary of faxing sensitive material. If a wrong fax number is input, your fax will go to that wrong number. Even when a fax is transmitted to the correct machine, it could be read by several people before your recipient has it in hand.

Voice Mail

Voice messages are considered forms of business communication. Although these are recorded communications, they are often treated as written messages. In many cases the caller first made a few notes before calling, and the listener is likely to write down important facts upon hearing it.

"The plane leaves Los Angeles International at 3:15 p.m., Flight 3458."

Make Your Voice Mail Heard

Many businesspeople receive a large number of voice messages each day, and it's possible that some will be ignored or forgotten. Here are some guidelines to help assure that your message will be one that is heard.

Identify Yourself

Start and end each voice message with your full name and contact information. If appropriate, include the name of your employer. Make it easy for your listener to call you back.

"This is Sam Johnston at Jones Lumber. Your order is ready for pickup. Let me know if you intend to send a truck or would prefer us to deliver it. If you want us to deliver it tomorrow, I'll need to hear from you before 4 p.m., today. Call me at 987-6543. Thanks."

Leave a Coherent—and Brief—Message

Long, windy voice messages are annoying, whether you receive one or many each day. To make sure that your message is one that will be heard, take the time to organize your thoughts before you dial. Make a few notes, if necessary, to be sure all details and salient points will be included in your message. If your message is longer than one minute, or if it includes too many details, it's too long. You need to send an e-mail or write a letter instead.

"Hi, Bill, this is Jill Engersmith. I've been researching Heyworth Wire, and I've come up with some interesting information on this company, including recent litigation over accounting irregularities. I'm preparing a detailed report on this, and I expect to have it on your desk by Thursday morning. If you want to discuss it now, give me a call. My extension is 6543. Thanks."

Speak Clearly

To be sure your message is understood, speak a bit more slowly than you might normally, and speak clearly. If you're calling from a cell phone, be sure there is ample cell coverage. Better to wait until you are in an area with sufficient coverage than leave a message that is mostly static.

Be Conscious of Voice Mail Security Issues

Remember that voice mail is not secure. There is no guarantee that the person you called will be the one listening to your message. Voice messages can be forwarded to another person's phone. Voice messages can be played back on a speaker phone—a situation where several people might be listening. A third party, perhaps an administrative assistant or other coworker, might be asked to pick up messages for the person you called. If you have sensitive information to relay, ask that your call be returned.

"Bill, this is Jerry. I'm concerned about the Caldwell situation, and I have a couple of ideas that might help. Give me a call when you get a chance. I'm at 123-555-7890. Thanks."

Part 3

*LETTERS
AND RESPONSES*

Ask About Prices and Discounts

Situation

Donna Rowe, Home Health nursing supervisor, wants to provide each of her visiting nurses with a handheld PDA (personal digital assistant). It is necessary that information gathered from home visits be easily downloaded to each nurse's computer as well as to the Home Health network. She contacts a distributor listed on the manufacturer's Web site.

Letter

Dear Mr. Wolfenberger:

We are considering providing each of our visiting nurses with a Wizard PDA. I saw a demonstration last week at the Medical Technology convention in Boise, and I think it would fill our needs very nicely.

I understand that the Model GH Wizard retails for $395. Do you offer a trade discount for organizations that buy in fairly large quantities? Our initial order would be for 35 units.

Please send me complete information, including pricing and discount information, service warranties, upgrade options, and extras, such as carrying cases.

Sincerely,

Response to a Request for Pricing Information

Situation

Paul Wolfenberger, sales representative for Wizard Products, replies to a letter from a potential customer. He wants to win this order, so he makes a personal phone call, then follows up with a letter.

Letter

Dear Ms. Rowe:

It was good talking to you earlier today, and I was most impressed by the good work that your organization offers to recently hospitalized patients and their families.

Our Web site is updated regularly and has complete details on the features of each model. I know you were interested initially in the GH model, but I would strongly recommend the CP model as a better choice for your nursing staff. The CP model has more memory, a bigger viewing screen, and is programmed with note-taking software. The CP model also comes with a hard plastic case at no extra charge.

Our standard discount is 10 percent on orders for 20 or more Wizards. Because this is your first order with Wizard, I can offer you an additional new customer discount of 5 percent, giving you a total savings of 15 percent on your initial order.

Thank you for your interest in the Wizard PDAs. If you need additional technical information or would like to use a CP model on a trial basis, give me a call. I look forward to speaking with you soon.

Cordially,

Ask About Training Materials

Situation

Leonard Ducey, Training Director of a large company, is setting up a series of communication seminars for supervisors and middle managers. At a recent professional meeting, Ducey heard a speaker refer favorably to a new multimedia program on communication skills. He first studied the Web site, then wrote to the author of the program.

Letter

Dear Mr. Rodriguez:

I was recently made aware that you had developed an excellent series of instruction modules on communication and management skills. According to your Web site, you also offer seminars to professional groups on these subjects.

I am setting up a series of communication workshops for our supervisors and middle managers. This year's series of in-house training sessions are scheduled for the first weeks of October, November, January, and February. Although we are considering purchasing several of your modules, we would like additional information on the workshops you conduct in person.

I look forward to hearing from you at your earliest convenience.

Sincerely,

Response to an Inquiry About Training Materials

Situation   Alfonso Rodriguez, a well-respected authority on communication and management skills, answers an inquiry about his multimedia programs available for purchase and the training seminars he conducts around the country.

Letter   Dear Mr. Ducey:

Thank you for your interest in my lectures and workshops. After talking to you on Tuesday, I am confident a one-day workshop on Supervisory Skills would be ideal for your group. This program has been used by hundreds of business firms and government agencies, and the reactions we've received have been most enthusiastic. I'm enclosing an outline of the topics covered.

The day starts with a lecture, then the rest of the morning is devoted to individual problem-solving exercises. After lunch, we'll continue with small-group training sessions and a final slide show. The fee also includes a kit of materials for each workshop participant.

We're in the process now of putting together a multimedia program on Salesmanship. The release date is scheduled for March of next year, so perhaps it would be suitable for your upcoming summer series of training sessions. I'll let you know when this new program is released.

Thanks again for your interest. As we discussed, you'll need to return the enclosed contract as soon as possible to guarantee your date on my schedule. I look forward to hearing from you.

Sincerely,

Ask for Appointment to See Networking Operation

Situation

George Mansfield is an accountant, and among his clients is a chain of six pharmacy stores. Mansfield is concerned about the increasing costs of record keeping in operating a pharmacy. A magazine article calls attention to new networking options designed specifically for pharmacies. Mansfield contacts the developer, requesting an appointment to learn more.

Letter

Dear Dr. Ruyle:

I was intrigued by your article in the June issue of *American Druggist*, and I am interested in learning more about the new networking options you discussed.

I have a client who could benefit greatly from these applications that your company developed specifically for pharmacies. Your system may be the answer to my client's problem, and I would like to learn more. I am particularly interested in seeing how it tracks and manages data reporting, as now required by the recent FDA mandates.

I will be in Seattle the week of August 18 and would very much like to see this system in operation. Please let me know if this will be convenient. I am scheduling appointments now, so I look forward to hearing from you soon. Thanks for your consideration.

Sincerely,

Invite Consumer to Software Demonstration

Situation

A software developer invites an interested consumer to see a demonstration of a new networking system. The developer wants to impress this person because he may well recommend this system to several of his clients.

Letter

Dear Mr. Mansfield:

We would be delighted to show you our latest pharmacy software package in action. If you are free the afternoon of August 20, we will take you to two pharmacies here in Seattle that have been using our network and are quite pleased with the results.

I'll schedule lunch for the two of us. After the site tour, I'd like you to meet with Ms. Sharon Tibbets, one of the primary developers of this software, so that she can answer any questions you may have.

We look forward to seeing you and offering a solution to your client.

Sincerely,

Ask for Detailed Information on a Service

Situation

The Executive Book Club has been running ads in several business magazines and other trade journals. Fritz Hoffman is interested in learning whether human resources administration is represented or whether there is a special book club for human resources executives. Hoffman writes to the contact name on the book club's Web site.

Letter

Dear Ms. Meyerson:

I notice that Executive Book Club advertises books that cover a wide spectrum of management issues. I need additional information before I join.

My main area of responsibility is Human Resources Administration. I would like to know what portion of the books that club members may choose from is in the field. If you have another book club that specializes in human resources, I would be very interested in learning more.

Thanks for any information you can provide.

Sincerely,

Supply Detailed Information on a Service

Situation   Priscilla Meyerson, member services administrator, responds to a request for more information about the Executive Book Club. She uses the opportunity to promote the cost savings for club members.

Letter   Dear Mr. Hoffman:

I am happy to answer your questions about our Executive Book Club.

Between 30 and 40 new books in the field of management are made available each year to club members. Looking at the current list, I see that 7 of our titles pertain specifically to Human Resources. In addition, there are quite a few general management books that embrace some aspect of HR administration.

Although we have specialized book clubs in accounting, computer science, and marketing, as yet we do not have one in human resources administration. The decision to set up a specialized book club is, of course, based on demand. Certainly there is a growing interest in this field, and we are currently researching the possibility of establishing an HR book club.

I'm enclosing a complete list of the books offered to club members. You will note that the average price of books distributed by Executive Book Club, if purchased separately, is over $40. However, members receive automatic discounts of 25 percent—or even more if the book is a featured monthly selection.

I hope this answers your questions. We would be happy to welcome you as a new member. Simply return the enclosed postcard or enroll on our Web site.

Sincerely,

Ask for Information About Dealers

Situation

Carefree Mobile Homes, Inc., placed an ad in *Mobile Homes Monthly*, offering information about a retail dealership. Richard Vannoy has been thinking about going into the mobile home business and writes to the company.

Letter

Dear Sirs:

Your ad in the January issue of *Mobile Homes Monthly* was intriguing. I have been researching the mobile home market, but have been unable to locate a dealer for Carefree Mobile Homes in the Atlanta area.

Also, I would like to learn more about Carefree Mobile Homes and their incentive program for dealers. Mobile homes are very popular in this area, and I am most interested in hearing more about your products and marketing opportunities.

Sincerely,

Response to Request from a Potential Dealer

Situation

Muriel Patterson, the director of marketing for Carefree Mobile Homes, responds to a potential dealer. She encloses information, recommends another dealer in the state, and introduces Carefree's sales representative.

Letter

Dear Mr. Vannoy:

Thanks very much for contacting us regarding becoming a dealer for Carefree Mobile Homes. The nearest dealer is Overton Homes in Savannah. The owner is Mrs. Muriel Overton, and I am certain she would be delighted to see you. Overton Homes has been one of our most successful outlets in Georgia and has a proven track record.

I'm enclosing a packet of information about Carefree Mobile Homes, including a detailed description of our entire product line and our generous incentive program for dealers. You can expect to hear soon from Bill Johnson, our sales representative. He tells me that he plans to be in your area two weeks from now.

I'm also enclosing a copy of an article, "Are Mobile Homes the Answer to the Nation's Housing Problem?" which appeared in a recent issue of *BusinessWeek*. I think you'll enjoy it.

Sincerely,

Complaint About Facility and Services

Situation

Frances Weller is manager of Lake Berry Hotel, which caters to groups of people attending conventions and meetings. Weller receives the following letter from Bryant Skinner, president of Pocono Realty Association, whose members recently completed a five-day stay at the hotel.

Letter

Dear Ms. Weller:

Because of the inefficiency of your staff, the fall meeting of the Pocono Realty Association was a big disappointment.

As you recall, the materials that were shipped to your hotel in advance for use in our group sessions were misplaced and not found until after our meetings had concluded. Our program had been built around these materials, and as a result of these being misplaced, we had to improvise. This was both awkward and unproductive.

We had paid our fee of $4,100 in advance, so there was no negotiating at the time of the conference. Still, I feel that we are entitled to some kind of reimbursement for the inconvenience we suffered. Please let me hear from you, as we will soon finalize our plans for next year's conference site.

Yours truly,

Response to Complaint About Facility and Services

Situation

Lake Berry Hotel did a poor job of hosting a conference. The hotel manager acknowledges the hotel's inefficiency and attempts to win back a disgruntled client.

Letter

Dear Mr. Skinner:

I am terribly embarrassed about the misplacement of your conference materials. I know this caused you many problems, and the fault was ours.

Lake Berry Hotel has consistently been rated number one in this area, and we'd like another chance to show you our best services. Your group has been coming here for the past four years, and we would be honored to welcome you again. To show that we mean what we say, Lake Berry is pleased to offer you a 15 percent discount on our conference facilities along with a 10 percent discount on hotel rooms booked by your members.

Our convention and banquet rooms are being remodeled this winter. At the same time, we're installing up-to-date multimedia equipment for use by our guests and conference attendees.

We would be delighted to welcome Pocono Realty Association again next year. I look forward to hearing from you at your earliest convenience.

Cordially,

Invitation to Tour Facility

Situation

LexRite Robotics has developed a new robotic assembly and tracking system for a medium-sized manufacturing company. The developers are confident that the system can be easily modified and adapted for other companies. The marketing director at LexRite arranges a demonstration for Marvin Goldsmith, a potential customer.

Letter

Dear Marvin,

I am pleased to invite you to tour our manufacturing facility next Thursday. We have arranged for a limo to pick up you and your associates at 9:30. We've planned a special luncheon for your group at the Omaha Club. Then we'll return to our conference center for a wrap-up meeting. We're sure to finish in plenty of time to beat the rush hour home.

We look forward to welcoming you and your team. Once you see our robotic system in operation at LexRite, I think you'll be excited about the possibilities for your company.

Sincerely,

Response to Invitation to Tour Facility

Situation   Marvin Goldsmith is interested in LexRite Robotics' latest assembly
system. LexRite has invited Goldsmith and his team to an on-site
demonstration. Goldsmith acknowledges the invitation and confirms the details.

Letter   Hi Bill,

We are looking forward to seeing the LexRite Robotics assembly and
tracking system in action. We're intrigued about the possible applications
for our products, so it should be a very productive day. Accompanying me
will be Angela, Max, and Don from my group, plus Marty and Bob from our
R&D department.

We'll be waiting for your limo Thursday morning, 9:30 sharp.

Best,

Invite a Panel Participant

Situation

As a leader of a panel discussion on advertising media at a convention, Fred Ferraro is inviting four experts to speak. The topic is advertising media—print, broadcast, direct mail, and Internet. The sponsoring organization will pay expenses for panel members plus a modest honorarium.

Letter

Dear Kara:

The Advertising Directors Guild will have its annual meeting September 4-6 at the Hilton in Washington, D.C. I have been asked to lead a panel discussion on Media Trends and Developments.

The panel will concentrate on four media—print, broadcast, direct mail, and Internet. A specialist for each medium will speak for about 15 minutes. These talks will be followed by a question-and-answer session where audience members can participate.

If you will be attending the meeting, would you serve as our expert on direct mail? ADG can offer you an honorarium of $200 to be a panel member. The media panel is scheduled for 2 p.m. to 4 p.m. on Tuesday, September 5.

I do hope you can undertake this assignment, and I'd appreciate your letting me know right away if you are available. If you want more information on past annual meetings, give me a call at the office. I'm looking forward to hearing from you.

Best,

Panel Participant's Polite Turn-Down

Situation

Kara Byrnes has been invited to be a member of a panel discussion on Media Trends and Developments. She declines the invitation due to previous commitments.

Letter

Dear Fred:

Thanks for the invitation to be on your panel at the ADG convention in September. Unfortunately, I'm already committed to another project, which will be coming to an end at that time.

If you don't have anyone else in mind, you might consider Professor Glenn Lane at the University of Hawaii. He is a dynamic speaker and a well-known specialist in direct mail marketing. If you decide to invite him, be sure to mention that I suggested him.

Have a good conference. I'm sorry to miss it.

Sincerely,

Invite a Professional Speaker

Situation

The chairperson of the program committee for the Travel Agents Association is seeking a speaker for the closing banquet. Several people have recommended Donna Kingsley as a good choice.

Letter

Dear Ms. Kingsley:

You have been highly recommended by several of our members as a speaker for the banquet that closes our annual three-day convention. This year's meeting will be held at the Sheraton Inn in Myrtle Beach, South Carolina. The date is the evening of October 3.

The banquet is purely a social affair, and we prefer an address on the light side but with an inspirational theme. I would leave it to you to select a topic that you feel would be appropriate for the occasion and audience.

Please let me hear from you by June 14. Be sure to include your fee and travel requirements along with program suggestions. I look forward to hearing from you.

Cordially,

Speaker's Response to Invitation

Situation

Donna Kingsley, a professional speaker, has been contacted by the Travel Agents Association to be a keynote speaker at their convention. She expresses her willingness to accept their invitation and presents her fee requirements.

Letter

Dear Ms. Wood:

I was very pleased to receive your invitation to be the keynote speaker on October 3, the closing day of the Travel Agents Association convention.

I have spoken twice to regional meetings of TAA, so I have had the pleasure of getting to know quite a few of your members. I have a slide show and speech entitled "Who Said Getting There Is Half the Fun?" It is a gentle spoof of the travel industry but ends with an inspirational note of generating understanding and unity around the world through travel. This talk has been well received by other organizations, and I'm confident your members will enjoy it as well.

My fee is $2,000 plus hotel and travel expenses. I'm enclosing my contract for your convenience. I urge you to reply as soon as possible because my calendar is filling quickly, and I can only hold the October 3 date for your group for another two weeks.

I look forward to hearing from you.

Cordially,

Confirming Speaker Contract

Situation

The program chairperson of the Travel Agents Association has contacted a professional speaker. The speaker's fees and other requirements are acceptable, and the program chairperson confirms the arrangement.

Letter

Dear Ms. Kingsley:

I am delighted you are available to be our keynote speaker on October 3.

Your signed contract is enclosed along with a copy of the hotel reservation. We will reimburse you for coach class airfare, but we do ask that you make your reservations right away in order to take advantage of lower rates. There is a free shuttle service between the airport and hotel. If you would prefer to have someone meet your plane, that can be arranged also.

Our social hour begins at 5 p.m. in the Pirate's Cove dining room. Please join me there and meet some of the association's officers and other members. Our after-dinner program starts at 7:30; you can expect to be introduced by 7:50.

We're very excited to have you as our closing speaker. Give me a call if I can do anything for you in advance.

Sincerely,

Poor Performance on Service Contract

Situation

An office building owner, Kathleen Malette, has a two-year contract with Universal Maintenance Service to provide janitorial services. There are ongoing complaints about poor service, and Malette has discussed the problem with the manager of Universal numerous times. The situation has not improved to Malette's satisfaction, and she writes to Universal, putting them on notice that the contract is in jeopardy.

Letter

Dear Mr. Weidner:

You will recall that you and I have had four discussions during the past six months about the low quality of service provided by your company. After each conversation, service improved for a short time, but soon declined as before.

Here is a summary of our previous discussions about your service:

- Windows. According to the contract, all windows are to be cleaned once a month. It has been eight weeks since the last window cleaning.

- Floors. All carpeted floors are to be vacuumed; tile and wood floors are to be washed and waxed. Your people have been vacuuming only. Tile floors are covered with black scuff marks.

- Furniture and Equipment. Furniture and equipment are to be dusted or vacuumed daily; desktops, chairs, and tables are to be cleaned and polished monthly. These duties are not being done satisfactorily. For example, ashtrays are often not emptied.

- Lavatories. These are to be cleaned and sanitized daily. Efforts here can only be described as careless.

If this matter cannot be resolved immediately, I will be forced to cancel our contract. In accordance with Section VIIc, which details provisions for revocation, this letter constitutes a final warning.

Sincerely,

Response to Complaint About Poor Service

Situation

John Weidner, the owner of Universal Maintenance Service, a janitorial service company, has received several complaints from one of his clients. Although he disagrees with many of the client's complaints, he does not quarrel with the customer. Instead he chooses to follow up personally to be sure that his workers are doing their job.

Letter

Dear Ms. Malette:

I will be inspecting your premises daily to be sure that my cleaning crew is doing a satisfactory job, and I will be sure that any shortcomings are corrected.

I believe this situation can be greatly improved, and I am determined to make it happen. Please accept my apologies, and let me know immediately if there is a problem that needs to be addressed.

Cordially,

Request Copy of Speech for Distribution

Situation

Dr. Carla Gomez recently spoke to the Phoenix chapter of the Arizona Management Association on the subject of incentive compensation. Her speech was enthusiastically received by the audience, and the Phoenix president, Mark Paulson, asked if he could make copies of her speech available to all Arizona chapters.

Letter

Dear Dr. Gomez:

Judging by the fine reception our members gave you, it's fair to say your presentation was simply outstanding.

I would like to have a copy of your speech that I can reproduce and send to other chapters in the Arizona Management Association. I am confident that other members will enjoy and profit by your remarks.

Thank you for your consideration.

Sincerely,

Sharing a Speech

Situation Dr. Carla Gomez was asked if a copy of her speech on incentive compensation could be distributed. Dr. Gomez is a professor of undergraduate business studies, and she is pleased to comply with the request.

Letter Dear Mark:

Here is a copy of my speech at the Phoenix chapter of the Arizona Management Association on October 7. Make as many copies as you like.

I only wish that all my lectures drew such favorable attention. Please extend my greetings to your members.

Sincerely,

Request Free Products

Situation

The National Association of School Superintendents is holding its annual convention in Atlantic City in August. Patricia Keating is preparing 500 "goodie bags" that will be given to all the people attending. Each bag includes free advertising materials, such as pens, small pads of paper, samples of hand cleaner, and the like. She writes to several companies and asks them for donations.

Letter

Dear Ward:

As you may know, the National Association of School Superintendents is holding its annual convention in Atlantic City this year. We are gathering products for a "goodie bag" to be given to everyone attending. We are expecting 500 attendees again this year.

In previous years you have donated ballpoint pens and pocket calendars. Will you do the same this year? Our members prize these items, and I see them continually in use during the convention. I understand that you are also an exhibitor at the convention, so this is also a good way to attract visitors to your booth.

Please send the materials to my attention. I'll need them by July 15. Thanks in advance for your donation.

Sincerely,

Response to Request for Free Products

Situation

Lopez School Supplies purchases exhibit space every year at the National Association of School Superintendents. As in previous years, the company donates products to be passed out to attendees as gifts. The sales manager writes a letter to the convention organizer to confirm this.

Letter

Dear Patricia:

Thank you for giving us this opportunity to help your organization and promote our products at the same time. This year I'm sending 500 pens and 500 key rings. I'm also sending flyers for you to include in the participants' kits. These flyers offer another freebie if they come to our booth during exhibit hours.

I'll be at the convention this year and am looking forward to seeing you once again. I'll be in the booth all day Friday, so perhaps you could stop by then.

Sincerely,

Request Marketing Information

Situation

To generate interest in its business gifts, a company takes an ad in the July issue of *Personnel International,* offering readers a free catalog. Jim Crandall, sales manager, wants to know what kind of response the ad generated.

E-mail

Bill,

How did the July ad in *Personnel International* do? Was the response as good as the June ad in *Human Resources Weekly*? I'd like to see a comparison of the responses to date from both ads.

Thanks,

Jim

Response to Request for Marketing Information

Situation

Bill Ferguson, promotion director, responds to the sales manager. As part of his job, Ferguson keeps track of ads and the responses each generates. He updates his records daily so that he can keep others informed as requested. In this instance, he replies immediately to the sales manager's inquiry.

E-mail

Jim,

The ad in *Personnel International* did better than we had hoped. We have had 357 requests to date through the 800 phone number. There was a blow-in postcard in that issue, and 250 have already been returned.

As you may recall, this is more than twice the response that we got from the *Human Resources Weekly* ad. Last month it pulled 150 phone requests and only 84 postcard returns.

Bill

Request Permission from Manager

Situation

Rita Barnes, manager of a bookstore, wants to know if she can stock a new book written by a local author. She contacts her regional manager, Jeanette Hines.

Letter

Jeanette,

I have a local author who's written a romance novel, and she's garnering a lot of publicity around here. I'd like to keep five to seven copies in stock, but I need your approval. *Love Along the Seine* by Marguerite Fischer will be available next month in paperback. The publisher is Reed Books. There is additional information on this at the publisher's Web site.

Thanks,

Response from Manager

Situation

The regional director of a bookstore chain has been asked if one of the bookstores in her region can stock a new book by a local author.

Letter

Dear Rita,

Reed Books is going to put some ad dollars behind this one, so start with six copies, then keep three on hand for the next six months.

After that, you'll have to order *Love Along the Seine* from our distributor. Because of your location, you should be able to fill any special requests within a day or two.

If this book looks like it's heading for the bestseller lists, let me know ASAP.

Best,

Request Permission to Reprint Unpublished Materials

Dr. C. B. Ogden would like to distribute copies of a speech he heard at a recent meeting of the Society of Chemical Engineers. He contacts the speaker and asks permission.

Letter

Dear Dr. Mangum:

I was greatly impressed with your remarks at the recent Society of Chemical Engineers meeting in Baton Rouge. Your experience in the TVA project made me realize that we at Bolling Chemical need to take a closer look at dry storage.

Is it possible to obtain a copy of your speech and make a dozen photocopies for our internal use? We're working on the problem of waste control, and I think your ideas would provide valuable guidelines for our research. We would not distribute the speech to anyone outside the company.

Thank you for your excellent presentation and for your consideration of this request.

Sincerely,

Deny Permission to Reprint

Situation

Dr. Cecil Mangum has been asked to give permission to have copies of a recent speech reprinted and distributed within a company. Although Dr. Mangum is not able to grant permission, he sends a friendly reply and offers another approach to obtaining reprint rights.

Letter

Dear Dr. Ogden:

Thank you for your interest in using my paper delivered at the recent Society of Chemical Engineers meeting. However, it is being published in a forthcoming issue of *Scientific Engineering,* and the magazine now owns publication and reprint rights.

Perhaps you might contact managing editor Clarence Musgrove in *Scientific Engineering*'s Los Angeles office. I am sure he can be of help in this matter.

Cordially,

Request Permission to Reproduce Illustration

Situation

Madeline Strong has been asked to do a presentation on annual reports. She is preparing handouts to distribute to attendees, and she wants to include a chart from a textbook. She asks permission from the publisher.

Letter

Dear Sirs:

I will be making a presentation on corporate annual reports at the regional convention of Financial Executives Association in Salt Lake City on March 5. I am preparing handouts for attendees; I expect an audience of approximately 75 people.

May I have permission to include the chart on page 425 of *Handbook of Public Relations*, Second Edition, by F. L. Selden. His structure for annual reports is well respected and widely used.

The handouts in which the chart will appear will be distributed free and only to those in attendance. I will make sure that full credit is given to the author and publisher. If you have a standard credit line that you require, I will be pleased to use it.

Thank you in advance for approving this request.

Cordially,

Grant Permission to Reproduce Illustration

Situation

A publisher has been asked to grant permission to reproduce an illustration from one of their business books.

Letter

Dear Ms. Strong:

You have our permission to reproduce the chart on page 425 of F. L. Selden's *Handbook of Public Relations*, 2/e.

Please use this credit line on the handout: "From *Handbook of Public Relations*, Second Edition, by F. L. Selden, HarperCollins, 2004."

We hope your presentation is well received, and we would appreciate receiving a copy of your handout when it is ready.

Sincerely,

Request Reprint Rights for Commercial Use

Situation   Matt Kaufman is preparing an employee training manual for franchise owners. These manuals will be given to the franchise stores. Kaufman asks the publisher for permission to reproduce one chapter of a book and offers a royalty fee.

Letter   Dear Mr. Smith:

I am preparing a training manual for retail sales employees in our 1,620 franchised stores throughout North America. The manual will be offered gratis to franchise owners for use in training employees.

I would like very much to include the excellent chapter "The Last Three Feet" from your book *Practical Sales Techniques*, Third Edition, by C. A. McFeister. We expect to distribute 12,000 copies a year and propose a royalty of $.05 on each copy. This would amount to $600 a year in royalties.

If this proposal is satisfactory, please sign and return the attached contract along with your requirements for copyright identification. We will not use your material in any other company publication without your permission.

Cordially,

Grant Reprint Rights

Situation

Vanguard Publications has received a request to reprint a chapter from one of their books. Even though the book is out of print, the publisher grants reprint rights.

Letter

Dear Mr. Kaufman:

The arrangements you suggested in your recent letter concerning reprint rights for Chapter 7 of C. A. McFeister's book are acceptable. The signed contract is enclosed.

The credit line on this section of your manual should appear as follows: "Reprinted by permission of C. A. McFeister from *Practical Sales Techniques*, Vanguard Publications, 2003. Further reproduction is prohibited."

Please forward four copies of your training manual when it is published.

Sincerely,

Request Reprints or Permission to Reproduce Magazine Article

Situation

Charles Maloney, marketing director of Pinnacle Products Corp., is planning the company's national sales conference with all sales personnel in attendance. Maloney is very impressed with an article that appeared in *Marketing Horizons.* He contacts the magazine for permission to reproduce and distribute the article.

Letter

Dear Mr. Taylor:

We are having our national sales conference in Birmingham the week of August 10. The theme this year is Winning Sales through Service. While researching this topic, I was much impressed with the article, "The Sale Doesn't End with the Order" by Cynthia O'Brien, which appeared in the May issue of *Marketing Horizons*.

Are reprints of this article available? If so, I would like 90 copies at your regular reprint rate. If reprints have not been made, I would like your permission to reproduce the article for sales conference attendees.

Cordially yours,

Give Permission to Reproduce Magazine Article

Situation

Philip Taylor, supervisor of subsidiary rights, grants limited permission to a corporation that wishes to distribute the article to sales conference attendees.

Letter

Dear Mr. Maloney:

Reprints of Cynthia O'Brien's article are not available, but you have our permission to reproduce 90 copies. Please add this credit line to the bottom of the first page: "Reproduced with permission of *Marketing Horizons*, May 2005, Cynthia O'Brien, author."

You have our best wishes for a successful sales conference.

Sincerely yours,

Solicit Solutions from Manufacturer

Situation

David Morgan, administrative services manager of Faultless Insurance Company, is researching modular cubicles so he can make maximum use of available office floor space. He contacts several manufacturers of custom office furniture, asking for their advice and recommendations.

Letter

Dear Sirs:

The rapid growth of our company has made office space a real problem in recent months. Rather than buy or lease additional space, we believe our immediate problem might be alleviated by making more efficient use of the space we now occupy.

We would be interested in having one of your experts visit our site and make recommendations. At that time, we can provide dimensions and current layouts of the three floors that we occupy in this building.

I look forward to hearing from you.

Sincerely,

Response to Request for Solutions

Michael Dewirth, manufacturer of custom office modules, responded to David Morgan's request for advice on making the best use of limited office space. After visiting Morgan's offices, Dewirth developed a new layout that he feels will solve Morgan's space problems. Dewirth invites Morgan and his associates to visit the showroom so they can inspect the products firsthand.

Letter

Dear David:

We are looking forward to having you visit our showroom next week. I think we've come up with a superior solution for your office space problems. We will be making a special presentation to you and your associates in the morning, then we'll tour the plant and display areas in the afternoon. Lunch will be in our executive dining room.

We'll pick you up at the Syracuse airport at 9:30 a.m. Our driver will be at door G3; he'll be holding a sign with your name, so you can't miss him.

I look forward to seeing you again.

Cordially,

Submit Draft for Approval

Situation

Pamela Voiles is Program Chairperson of the Association of Life Underwriters, which is having its annual convention three months from now. Pamela has designed the membership booklet, but needs approval of the association's president, Carl Martin, before having it printed.

Letter

Dear Carl:

At last all the pieces of the membership booklet have been prepared, and I'm ready to have it printed as soon as you give your okay. A sample copy is enclosed.

- Format and fonts are the same as in previous years; only the color of the cover has changed. This year's cover is antique gold paper with dark brown ink. The logo will be centered at the top of the cover as before.

- The association bylaws are now in the back of the booklet.

- The programs and speakers for this year's monthly meetings are in the front of the booklet.

- Jack Mobley has been taking pictures of members at each meeting. These are a nice addition to the names and contact information.

- I plan to print 500, more than enough for our membership. The cost of the additional 150 copies was nominal.

If you have any changes, let me know. I will be turning this over to the printer on February 5.

Thanks,

Approve a Draft

Situation

Carl Martin has been asked to approve a booklet for an association. He makes some suggestions and gives his approval.

Letter

Dear Pamela:

Thanks for letting me see the mock-up of the membership booklet. Please make the following two changes before going to press:

- Put board information—names, e-mail addresses, phone numbers—on the inside front cover.

- Put a splashy ad about the upcoming convention on the inside back cover.

By using the blank cover pages, the text page layouts won't change.

Best,

Part 4

CREDIT AND
COLLECTION LETTERS

Accept Applicant for Commercial Credit

Situation

Johnson & Hall, a wholesale auto parts distributor, receives an order and request for short-term credit from Live Oak Auto Parts, a new retail store owned by J. C. Laughlin. The information supplied by Laughlin and his credit references is very favorable. The wholesaler welcomes Laughlin as a credit customer and encourages him to use the privilege frequently.

Letter

Dear Mr. Laughlin:

It is a pleasure to welcome you as a credit customer of Johnson & Hall. Credit terms are described in detail on the enclosed sheet.

We will be sending you our monthly newsletter *Auto Spotlight,* which will give you up-to-date information on everything new in automotive parts.

We look forward to serving you and hope you will call upon us often. In the meantime, we wish you outstanding success at Live Oak Auto Parts.

Sincerely yours,

Accept Applicant for Consumer Credit

Situation

After moving to Atlanta, Sylvia Chin applied for credit at Fitch's Finery, a popular and respected department store. She easily met all requirements for receiving credit and is welcomed by the credit manager as a "select" customer.

Letter

Dear Ms. Chin:

Enclosed is your Fitch's Finery Gold Card, which I am delighted to send you. This credit card can be used in person, when ordering by phone, or when shopping online.

In addition, our Gold Card members are entitled to special privileges. You can take advantage of sales the day before they are open to the general public. You can also use our Personal Shopper Service at no extra charge. And finally, Gold Card members will be offered special discounts on select merchandise each month.

Fitch's Finery is pleased to welcome you as a Gold Card member. The next time you're in our store, bring this letter to Customer Service. There's a special gift waiting there for you.

Sincerely yours,

Customer Receives Collection Letter in Error

Situation

Duvall Tools purchases hardware from Michigan Supply Corp. Duvall receives a warning that if the company does not pay their bill in full, their account will be suspended. Duvall has already paid this bill and owes nothing. The accounts payable manager at Duvall Tools contacts Michigan Supply Corporation to confirm this.

Letter

Dear Rob,

Please update your records to show that Duvall's account has been paid in full.

A copy of our canceled check is enclosed. Note that our check was dated February 3 and endorsed by Michigan Supply Corporation on February 12. Our policy is to pay our bills within 10 days of receipt, which we did do in this case.

If you have any questions, give me a call.

Sincerely,

Response to Complaint About Collection Letter

Situation

Michigan Supply Corporation's accounts receivable manager recently sent a warning letter to Duvall Tools regarding a balance due on their account. The letter had been sent in error, and Michigan Supply Corporation notifies Duvall Tools that their account is once again in good standing.

Letter

Dear Bill:

This is to confirm that the Duvall Tools account is in good standing with a zero balance as of February 13.

I do apologize for the warning letter. Duvall has been a good customer for many years and it shouldn't have been sent. Thanks for your help in getting this straightened out.

Sincerely,

First Reminder After Monthly Statement

Situation

On February 3, Greenacres Nursing Home purchases supplies and equipment from Walton Medical Supply Company on 30-day credit terms. Although the nursing home has been in operation only a short time, the information concerning the enterprise has been favorable and credit was granted.

A regular statement is mailed on March 10. When no response is received by March 20, a second statement is sent.

First Reminder—Past Due Statement

Walton Medical Supply Co.
744 Perry Avenue
Davenport, Iowa 52801
(800) 555-6308

Statement

PAST DUE AMOUNT

To: Greenacres Nursing Home
P. O. Box 888
Rolla, MO 65401
Attn: Glenn Montgomery

Date	Invoice No.	Past Due Amount
09/06/05	Y-2114	$2,195.35

PLEASE REMIT IN FULL.

Second Reminder After Monthly Statement

Situation

Greenacres Nursing Home makes no response to the Past Due statement. Ten days later a second reminder is sent. A copy of the Past Due statement is attached to the reminder letter.

Second Reminder— Letter

Dear Mr. Montgomery:

To date no payments have been received from you, and we are assuming that this is merely an oversight on your part. Please remit the full past due amount immediately.

If your payment of $2,195.35 has already been sent, we thank you.

Sincerely,

Third Reminder After Monthly Statement

Situation

Greenacres Nursing Home still has not responded to the previous reminders. A third reminder is sent 10 days after the second one. Again, a copy of the Past Due statement is attached to the letter.

Third Reminder— Letter

Dear Mr. Montgomery:

Is there some reason we have not yet received payment from you? The amount owed is long past due, and we are concerned. Please let us hear from you at once. Or, simply remit payment in full in the amount of $2,195.35.

Yours truly,

Fourth Reminder After Monthly Statement

Situation

The credit manager at Walton Medical Supply Company, Bethany Kroll, has heard nothing from Greenacres Nursing Home, and the bill is now 30 days past due. She places a telephone call to the owner. Because he is not available, she leaves a voice mail message.

Fourth Reminder— Voice Mail

"Hello, Mr. Montgomery. This is Bethany Kroll at Walton Medical Supply Company, and I'm calling to remind you about your past due bill of $2,195.35. As you know, this invoice is now over 30 days past due. Please remit immediately so that your good standing with us is not in jeopardy. If you have any questions, call me at (800) 555-1764.

"Thank you."

Fifth Reminder After Monthly Statement

Situation

Glenn Montgomery of Greenacres Nursing Home received a voice message from Walton Medical Supply and returned the call, promising to remit payment immediately, but no payment has been received. A stern reminder is sent via Priority Mail.

Fifth Reminder— Priority Mail Letter

MR. MONTGOMERY:

PER OUR CONVERSATION OF APRIL 12, YOU PROMISED IMMEDIATE PAYMENT OF YOUR ACCOUNT IN THE AMOUNT OF $2,195.35. YOUR CHECK HAS NOT ARRIVED, AND IF IT IS NOT ALREADY IN THE MAIL, I URGE YOU TO SEND IT TODAY.

REMIT PAYMENT IN FULL WITHIN 7 BUSINESS DAYS OR WE WILL BE FORCED TO PROCEED WITH LEGAL ACTION.

BETHANY KROLL, CREDIT MANAGER
WALTON MEDICAL SUPPLY

Sixth and Final Reminder After Monthly Statement

Situation

Because Greenacres Nursing Home neither sent payment nor called with an explanation, Walton Medical Supply sends notification that the account will be turned over to a collection agency.

Sixth and Final Reminder— Letter

Mr. Montgomery:

This is our final reminder.

We must receive payment in full in the amount of $2,195.35 by May 1. If not, your account will be placed in the hands of our attorneys for collection.

Yours truly,

Offer Credit to New Customer

Situation

Bayside Building Supply has just sold a large order for lumber and other materials to Ernest Lacy, a new contractor in town. Bayside writes to Lacy, encouraging him to establish a credit account.

Letter

Dear Mr. Lacy:

Thank you for your recent business. We have been suppliers for many contractors for over 60 years. With the current building boom still in progress, the future looks bright.

We want you to know that credit privileges are available here at Bayside Building Supply. We require three local references, a statement from the Better Business Bureau, and credit reports from both your bank and a credit agency.

The next time you're here, let me know. I'd be pleased to tell you about some of the other special services that are available exclusively to our charge customers.

Sincerely,

Request Commercial Credit

Situation

The Computer Place not only sells computer equipment, but also provides computer services to local businesses. At a recent business show, the owner of The Computer Place, Gretchen Rivera, saw a computer printer that sells for $875. She thinks it will be a popular item for the businesses she serves, and she writes to the manufacturer requesting credit terms.

Letter

Dear Sirs:

When I visited the Omaha Business Show last week, I saw your new Harrison-Fisher Laser Jet 4 printer. I think this printer would meet the need of many of my customers.

I would like to order three LJ4s on 60-day credit terms and at the same time establish similar terms for future purchases up to $5,000 monthly. As I understand it, the printer is priced at $1,100 plus $50 for transportation, terminal checkout, and one ream of paper. This means that my first order would amount to $3,450.

The Computer Place was established two years ago, and since that time we have grown very rapidly. My associates and I are convinced that the services and equipment we offer will be in increasing demand as businesses discover that only by applying sophisticated technology to their operations can they remain competitive.

For information concerning our financial responsibility and promptness in paying our obligations, I refer you to the following:

First National Bank, 106 East Mitchell Street, Wichita KS 67202
Rotec, Inc., 6200 Newman Avenue, Huntington Beach, CA 92647
Allied Data Associates, 4406 Cromwell Drive, El Paso, TX 79912
Winthrop Systems, 16536 Brick Avenue North, Seattle, WA 98133

If you would like additional financial information, I will be glad to supply it.

Very truly yours,

Request Information from a Commercial Credit Applicant

Situation

Upon receipt of the order and credit application from The Computer Place, the manufacturer responds promptly and with appreciation. However, in recent years many computer stores have gone out of business very quickly. The manufacturer decides to tactfully ask the credit applicant for additional financial information.

Letter

Dear Ms. Rivera,

Thank you very much for your interest in our Harrison-Fisher Laser Jet 4 printers. This instrument was designed with the small business in mind, and I think your assessment of it is right on target.

I also appreciate your request to purchase three LJ4s on 60-day credit terms and to establish similar terms for future purchases. The references you supplied will be very helpful.

Would you please send me a copy of your most recent statements of ownership and results of operations? Or, if you prefer, you can use the enclosed forms to supply the required data.

You may be sure, Ms. Rivera, that just as soon as we have the information we need, we'll attend to your request. We're eager to have the LJ4s in the hands of your customers, and we'll do our best to expedite shipment.

Very cordially yours,

Request Information from References

Situation

The manufacturer of the HF Laser Jet 4 printer writes to the references supplied by The Computer Place. The same letter was sent to each reference.

Letter

Dear _____:

We have received a request for credit privileges from The Computer Store, owned by Ms. Gretchen Rivera. Your company was listed as a credit reference.

I would be very grateful if you would supply the following information about this customer:

1. Credit terms extended to this customer, including limits:

   _____

2. A brief statement concerning the customer's promptness in meeting obligations:

   _____
   _____
   _____

3. Your reservations, if any, about the customer's financial condition and general reliability:

   _____
   _____
   _____

I assure you that the information supplied will be treated with the strictest confidence. Thank you for your assistance.

Sincerely,

Turn Down Applicant for Commercial Credit

Situation

Rhodes Furniture receives an order from Premier Career Academy for classroom furniture in the amount of $4,800 and asking for 24-month credit terms. The financial statement supplied indicates the school's economic situation is very shaky. The credit manager of Rhodes Furniture writes a turn-down letter.

Letter

Dear Ms. Ashford:

Thank you for your recent order #9725 in which you requested credit terms of 24 months.

Unfortunately, the information you supplied was not at all favorable concerning the financial condition of Premier Career Academy. Under the circumstances, we must defer credit privileges at this time.

We can, however, offer you a 3 percent discount for cash payment. Please remit a cashier's check for $4,656 ($4,800 less 3 percent) and we will expedite your order immediately.

Cordially,

Turn Down Applicant for Consumer Credit

Situation

Kermit Greene applied to Richter's Department Store for a store credit card. Greene's credit report reveals that he has a long history of making late payments on other credit cards, so the store turns down his request.

Letter

Dear Mr. Greene:

Thank you for your interest in establishing a charge account at Richter's. After careful consideration, we must turn down your application. When your financial picture improves, we would be pleased to have you reapply for store credit.

In the meantime, it will be a pleasure for us to welcome you as a cash customer. If you'd like advance notice of special sales, visit our Web site and give us your e-mail. We'll keep you posted on all upcoming store events.

We look forward to serving you.

Cordially,

Turn Down Retail Applicant for Credit

Situation

Blue Moon Camera has in the past ordered supplies from Zebulon Suppliers, a wholesaler of camera equipment and supplies, but always on a cash basis. The latest order is in the amount of $2,400, and Blue Moon's owner, Karl Moran, asks for credit. The references submitted by Blue Moon indicate that the store is not a good credit risk. The credit manager at Zebulon denies credit privileges but attempts to maintain goodwill with this customer.

Letter

Dear Mr. Moran:

Thanks for supplying credit information about your store. Unfortunately, I must turn down credit privileges at this time. However, please apply again when your financial picture has improved.

In the meantime, I hope you will find it possible to continue to order from us on a cash basis. We are proud of our products and our services. As always, we will continue to do everything possible to see that you get what you want when you want it.

Sincerely yours,

Part 5

MORE SAMPLE LETTERS

Acknowledge Illness

Situation

Robert Harrell has been diagnosed with a serious illness that will require extensive medical treatment. Sheila Ferguson, a client, learns of his illness and writes to express her concern.

Letter

Dear Bob:

I was distressed to hear about your recent diagnosis. However, Kitty said that the surgery went well and your chemo treatments will begin in another week.

She also said that you were a patient at the University of Indiana. That was wonderful news, as I know that their teaching hospital and medical facilities are rated among the best in the country.

For now, follow your doctor's orders, and take advantage of the time off to catch up on your crossword puzzles. You have lots of friends, and we're all sending get well wishes your way.

Sincerely,

Acknowledge Large Order

The sales representative for Pathfinder Publishing has just received an order from Mrs. Cynthia Eulan for accounting textbooks. The order is larger than expected and the salesman writes to Mrs. Eulan, thanking her for the order.

Letter

Dear Cynthia:

I was delighted to receive your order for 215 copies of *Accounting Principles*. These textbooks have been very popular and I'm glad that you agree. Other teachers have reported that the text is comprehensive in coverage, yet well-organized and easy for students to use.

To make your preparation easier, we also offer supplementary materials for this textbook, including workbooks, transparencies for overhead projectors, and unit tests. I'm enclosing some sample pages and transparencies from Chapter 3 of the workbook that accompanies the text.

I understand that you'll also be using textbooks for the evening accounting program. We have a full line of supplementary materials prepared especially for adult education classes.

Please let me know if I can be of further service.

Cordially,

Acknowledge Reader's Suggestion

Situation

Capital Cities Forest Industries recently ran a series of advertisements in several national publications. The responses to these ads have been highly favorable. The public relations department answers many of the letters of accolade they receive.

Letter

Dear Ms. Parkinson:

You were very thoughtful to write praising our series of forestry ads in *Rocky Mountain Monthly*. We are pleased that you find these ads provocative and stimulating.

Your suggestion that we give more emphasis to creatures of the wild is very appropriate. The next series of six ads will emphasize the importance of protecting our wildlife, especially endangered species. I'm sure you'll find this series equally informative.

Sincerely,

Announce Acquisition

Situation

Payne-Wyatt recently purchased Rothmore-Medico, a relatively small but prestigious publisher of both textbooks and professional publications in the medical field. Payne-Wyatt sends the announcement to all employees of both companies.

Announcement

To: All employees

Payne-Wyatt is pleased to announce the acquisition of Rothmore-Medico, a longtime publisher of medical textbooks and related materials for physicians.

We are immensely proud of this union of two important publishing houses. Rothmore-Medico was founded in 1932 by Douglas H. Rothmore, a distinguished medical professional. Rothmore-Medico, long recognized as one of the country's preeminent medical publishers, recently launched *Medical Innovations,* a sophisticated monthly magazine with a circulation of over 100,000 readers, to health-care professionals, libraries, and hospitals.

We welcome Rothmore-Medico into the Payne-Wyatt group. Michael Beyer will continue as president of Rothmore, reporting to Payne-Wyatt CEO Clark Trimple. We want to assure everyone that no employee layoffs are expected at this time. Rothmore-Medico employees will be moving into the Payne-Wyatt building on Lexington Avenue over the next few months.

Announce Anniversary

Situation

TimePlus Watch Company will celebrate its seventy-fifth anniversary in May. To commemorate the occasion, the president writes to retail store owners offering a special bonus.

Letter

Dear Ms. Fisher:

In May, TimePlus will observe its seventy-fifth anniversary, an occasion we think deserves a celebration. Morton Reed, the founder of TimePlus, was among the first to promote the change from pocket and pendant watches to wristwatches for men and women, young and old.

To commemorate this event, we are offering a special collector's edition of Morton Reed's original watch. The watch is round with a gold face and has an attractive black leather wristband. Roman numerals are at 3, 6, and 9. Twelve is marked with a small ruby. The anniversary reproduction is engraved with Reed's signature on the back of the case.

Only 7,500 of these seventy-fifth anniversary watches will be produced. Each will be numbered and boxed in a special red velvet presentation case. The suggested retail price is $750. The watch will be shipped to dealers on May 1. Orders received before January 1 will receive an additional discount of 15 percent off the dealer price. This special discount is good for only four more weeks, so act now. Fax your order to 1-800-555-4566, or order online at the TimePlus Web site.

Best regards,

Announce Appointment

Situation

DeWitt J. Fuller has just been appointed senior consultant in small business management at Harlan Thomas Associates. The company sends a press release to several business trade journals as well as newspaper business editors.

Press Release

For immediate release

DeWitt J. Fuller Joins Harlan Thomas Associates

DeWitt J. Fuller, former manager of New Orleans Small Business Administration field office, has joined Harlan Thomas Associates as senior consultant in small business management.

Fuller will provide special counsel to those who are considering starting a business as well as those who are already operating a business and need assistance in financial planning, marketing strategies, and general management techniques.

President R. B. Myers stated, "Small business owners have largely been neglected by management consulting organizations, and we are convinced that an enormous contribution can be made by our company, not only to the owners themselves, but to the business community as a whole. We feel very fortunate in having a person with Fuller's experience to head up this important new service."

Fuller is the author of *Successful Small Business Management* (Ploughman Press) and numerous articles in business trade journals.

Announce Hiring Freeze

Situation

Winsted Corporation is concerned about the poor profit picture during the past six months. Expenses must be cut, and a freeze on hiring is announced. The company president notifies all division managers that there is now a moratorium on staff additions.

Memo

To: All Division Managers

From: Joseph Barrington, President

Subject: Moratorium on Staff Additions

Effective immediately, there will be no staff increases during the next two fiscal quarters. This includes temporary employees as well as new hires. This decision stems from our dismal profits in the first two quarters of the year. We must reduce expenses wherever possible no matter how much it hurts.

Employees who leave the company during the next six months will not be replaced. I realize this may be a genuine hardship in some divisions, but let's see if we can reorganize as required to avoid hiring replacements. All pending requisitions for new hires and permanent temps are canceled.

I'm willing to listen if you believe these restrictions promise catastrophe in your department, but be aware that deviations from this policy will be hard to sell.

Announce Meeting

Situation

Jim Montgomery, vice president of human resources, is concerned about training for new employees. He notifies his department managers about a meeting. The objective is to have the group come up with more effective ways to welcome new employees in the company.

Letter

Dear _____:

We have been conducting orientation workshops for new employees for some time now. These occur every other month, and the purpose is to acquaint new employees with the company. Feedback from participants suggests that our present workshops are lifeless and humdrum.

Let's meet on February 10 at 9:30 a.m. in Conference Room A.

Be prepared to suggest ways to make these workshops more interesting and productive, including a new format, better media presentations, and employee participation. These workshops are a golden opportunity for us to build esprit de corps among our new hires, and we shouldn't be wasting it.

Thanks,

Announce New Library

Situation

Avery Chemical Corporation has established a company library, open to all employees regardless of position or rank. Eileen R. Burke, vice president of research and development, announces the library and its services.

Announcement

To: All Employees

From: Eileen R. Burke, vice president, Research and Development

Subject: Library Open House

The company library is now completed and available for use by all employees. There will be an Open House during the day on November 5, and all are invited to drop by at their convenience. Refreshments will be served.

Here are some of the highlights of our new library:

Books. We stock business and professional books in many areas, with the emphasis on chemistry and related fields. Our reference shelf includes scientific manuals as well as a variety of specialized dictionaries.

Periodicals. We subscribe to the popular business magazines, including *BusinessWeek, Forbes, Fortune*, and more. We also have publications from various technical, professional, and engineering societies.

Catalogs. We have a very large file of manufacturers' catalogs, including those of our competitors. We keep unbound pamphlets, news clippings, and other trade resources that you will find useful.

Company records. We have a complete file of Avery Chemical Corporation's history, including annual reports.

Additional services. Our staff can arrange library loans and the use of facilities of local and regional libraries. We can also assist employees in the preparation of technical articles for publication.

Our head librarian is Martha Lennon; assistants are Melba Crutchfield, Mike Bryan, and Marie McSpadden. The library will be open during regular office hours—9 a.m. to 5 p.m., Monday through Friday. They look forward to working with you.

Announce New Location

Situation

R&J Equipment Rentals has occupied rental space in downtown Baltimore for nearly 10 years. Recently the firm constructed its own building in Glen Burnie, a suburb of Baltimore. R&J announces the change of location to its many customers and to suppliers in the vicinity.

Announcement

R&J EQUIPMENT RENTALS, INC.
323 Eastwood Road
Glen Burnie, MD 21061
(800) 555-4567

We've moved to Glen Burnie! Come visit us in our new facility. More room, more equipment, same excellent service.

- Air Compressors
- Welding Machines
- Masonry Saws
- Vibrators
- Pumps

- Scaffolds
- Forklifts
- Mortar Mixers
- Electric Hand Tools
- Concrete Accessories

Announce New Products and Services

Situation

Holliman's Office Supplies, a leading office supply store in Cheyenne, Wyoming, recently became the exclusive distributor of a line of copying machines. The store sends a promotional announcement to attract new customers.

Announcement

YOU'VE GOT THE DILEMMA? WE'VE GOT THE SOLUTION!

Holliman's Office Supplies, for over 50 years Cheyenne's leading office supply store, is proud to announce that they are now the exclusive distributor of Caldwell Imaging Systems.

Caldwell products reflect the latest developments in imaging systems. They offer the very best in toner photocopiers, color copiers, digital images, laser printers, and image storage and retrieval systems. Caldwell's Model 3200 series gives your company publishing capabilities.

We support Caldwell's products with our own factory-trained technicians, on call around the clock. Give us a call at (800) 555-4567.

Announce Plans for New Warehouses

Situation

Hanover Plastics has decided to build three new warehouses. Ben Fisher, executive vice president, confirms the company plans to the operations committee.

Memo

To: Operations Committee

From: Ben Fisher

Subject: Warehouse Specs

Reese Builders has been chosen to build new warehouses for us in Schenectady, Pittsburgh, and Fort Wayne. Reese's planning specialists will be here the week of April 11 to study our specific requirements.

They are particularly interested in our procedures for receiving, storing, and shipping our products. We'll need an updated estimate of our space needs in each of our three locations. Please examine your earlier reports and revise as needed. I'll need your new estimates by April 6.

It is very important that you and your principal warehouse supervisors be available for individual conferences with the Reese people. If for any reason you will be unavailable April 11-13, please let me know right away.

Thanks,

Announce Promotion

Situation
Edward Whitten, formerly editor-in-chief, is promoted to vice president and editorial director of Blackstone Publishing. The announcement of this promotion is sent to executives, managers, and editors.

Announcement

To: Corporate and Division Executives, Managers, and Editors

From: Benjamin Feldman, CEO

Subject: Appointment of Edward R. Whitten

Edward R. Whitten is appointed vice president and editorial director, effective March 1. This announcement is made with great pleasure and satisfaction.

Blackstone has long been a major publisher of educational and business materials. Our leadership in this field is due to the high standards that have made us famous. Ed Whitten will be expanding our role into two vital publishing areas—medicine and industrial construction. Reporting to Whitten will be Editing Services, Copyrights and Permissions, and Production Research.

Ed Whitten grew up in Oklahoma, graduated cum laude from Oklahoma State University, and in that state began his professional life as a school teacher. He worked briefly as a sales representative for Payne-Wyatt and was associate dean of Beacon College in Richmond, California. As editor-in-chief, he has had a major hand in bringing Blackstone Publishing to editorial eminence in business education.

Announce Sale of Office Equipment

Situation

Star Life Insurance Company recently purchased new office furniture and equipment. The old furniture and equipment is offered to employees first. Whatever is left will be sold to a used furniture dealer.

Announcement

To: All Employees

We've just filled up Warehouse B with lots of used—but still serviceable—office equipment and furniture. All of it is available for purchase by employees on a first-come, first-served basis.

Need a file cabinet at home? We have 16 in very good condition. Desks? We have 22 of those. We've got chairs, bookcases, lamps, and 36 inspirational pictures.

And don't forget equipment. This is a good chance to pick up a perfectly good computer for your home office. We've got 36 calculators, 4 faxes, 7 scanners, and 2 large light tables.

The warehouse is open from 8 a.m. to 6 p.m. These sales are rare, so take advantage now. But hurry—our sale ends next week.

Apologize for Inconveniences

Situation   When Super Supplies builds a new store in the suburbs, President Karl Fisk writes a letter to residents in the area, apologizing for the inconveniences of the building and offering them a special discount.

Letter   Dear Hawthorne Hills resident:

Building a new store can be a complicated project. We have tried to minimize the nuisance and discomfort for our friends, but we recognize that any large development like the new Super Supplies being built in your area is bound to cause some inconvenience.

We think you'll be proud of this new Super Supplies outlet—a full acre of shopping pleasure. Our grand opening is April 10, and we'd love to have you attend our open house that day. There will be entertainment, balloons for the children, and special snacks for all.

To show our appreciation for your patience during the building process, we are enclosing a special discount coupon, good for 25 percent off any item in our store. Visit us soon. We want to welcome you to the Super Supplies family of smart shoppers.

Sincerely,

Confirm Oral Instructions

Situation

Several retail customers of Woodmere Paint Company have recently complained about defective spray nozzles on VelvetCoat, a popular brand of enamel. Helen Gilbert, a store manager, phoned Woodmere's adjustment department, saying it was too costly to return the paint and that credit should be granted solely on the retailer's word. Woodmere manager, Leslie Louis, agrees with Gilbert and confirms their conversation with a letter.

Letter

Dear Helen:

This is to confirm our discussion about not returning the VelvetCoat spray nozzle cans. I agree with you completely, and we'll take your word that the cans are faulty. Just tell us how many you have had to replace.

Meanwhile, we're investigating the problem. This has never happened before, and we're trying to determine the source of the defect so we can correct it immediately.

Thanks again for your input.

Cordially,

Confirm Prices and Discounts

Situation

Ronald Rietzke is a salesman for a building supply corporation. He received a call from Joseph Minor, a retailer, asking about prices on Modu-Screen acoustical partitions. Rietzke quoted the prices on the telephone, then confirmed them in writing.

Letter

Dear Mr. Minor:

Thank you for your call this morning. This will confirm our conversation about costs for Modu-Screen acoustical partitions. The prices apply to all colors available in acrylic partitions. Frames and matching end legs and top caps are included in the price.

Partition Dimensions	Price, each	Price, each, 12 or more
4' × 4', straight	$122.75	$98.20
4' × 5', straight	$132.00	$115.50
5' × 5', straight	$152.75	$129.85
5' × 5', curved	$191.00	$152.80

If you order through our Web site, we offer an additional 5 percent discount on orders of 12 or more. I would urge you to place your order soon, as we are expecting that prices will be somewhat higher after July 31.

Thank you for your interest in our partitions. I look forward to receiving your order.

Cordially,

Confirm Travel Arrangements

Situation

Charles Winthrop, president of Worldwide Music, has invited J. D. Folsom, the owner of four music stores, to visit Worldwide's plant in Shreveport, Louisiana. Winthrop has offered to pay for travel and other expenses. Folsom accepted the invitation, and the date for the visit is set for April 14. Winthrop plans the itinerary and confirms the arrangements.

Letter

Dear J.D.:

I'm looking forward to giving you a tour of our brass manufacturing facility, then showing you around Shreveport. Here's the itinerary for your arrival Tuesday:

Air Travel

Leave Wilmington, 11:30 a.m., USAir 220
Arrive Atlanta, 1:30 p.m.

Leave Atlanta, 3:15 p.m., Delta 416
Arrive Shreveport, 5:15 p.m.

Hotel

Best Western Chez Vous Motor Inn
317 Frontage Road, Shreveport
(800) 555-7890

Plane tickets are enclosed. I will meet you at the airport and take you to the motel. Kate Jackson and Harold DiGarmo will be joining us for dinner at the Sunset Palace restaurant.

Cordially,

Congratulate Coworker

Situation   When a friend, coworker, or superior in your company receives a promotion, it is always prudent to write a personal note of congratulations.

Letter

Dear Stan:

Your promotion to vice president of Human Resources was great news. I was really quite pleased to hear that you are now in charge.

It's nice to see that the company is implementing a policy of promoting from within. It's encouraging for us all to see talent rewarded.

Sincerely,

Congratulate Employee for Years of Service

Situation

Robbins Metals Corporation honors employees who have worked for the company for 25 years. The president writes a letter of congratulation to honor the employee and express appreciation for loyal service.

Letter

Dear Sidney:

I consider it a distinct privilege to congratulate you on the completion of 25 years at Robbins Metals Corporation and to invite you to become a member of the Twenty-Five Year Club.

This is an important group of employees, for it is they who have contributed the most to our growth and to our good name. I hope you look back on these years with great satisfaction and pride. It's a significant achievement, and I want to express my personal appreciation for your loyalty and contribution.

Enclosed is our invitation to the annual Twenty-Five Year Club dinner. I look forward to seeing you there and congratulating you in person on becoming a member of this very exclusive group.

Best regards,

Congratulate Employee on Anniversary

Situation

Martha Olson, purchasing director, is well respected by other employees for her managerial skills and knowledge of the industry. It is now her fifteenth anniversary with the company and the president writes her a personal letter expressing his appreciation.

Letter

Dear Martha:

I just wanted to congratulate you on being with Atlantic Mills for 15 years. In every job you've had here, you were held in high esteem by your coworkers for your professional expertise and leadership skills.

As we continue to grow, the purchasing function will have an increasingly important role at Atlantic Mills. I hope you anticipate the challenge. Certainly there's no doubt in my mind that you will rise to it.

Best regards,

Congratulate Employee on a Job Well Done

Situation

Louise Langan, an employee in the information technology group, receives a letter of appreciation from the vice president of her division. Louise was instrumental in the development of a new system for tracking automobile insurance claims nationwide.

Letter

Dear Louise:

Thank you for your contribution to making the Claims Tracking Network so successful. I understand that your initial specifications were important in getting our programmers on the right track from the get-go. In addition to your programming skills, your knowledge and expertise regarding the auto claims industry has been invaluable. We estimate that this system will save our clients millions of dollars each and every year. Under your leadership, this program has become the most effective instrument of its kind.

Again, I want to express my deep appreciation for your efforts. It is employees like you that make this company number one in the industry.

Warmest regards,

Congratulate Employee on New Procedure

Situation

Morris Symonds, manager of a manufacturing plant, implements a new system for communication between shifts. It has been working very well, and the vice president of operations writes to compliment Symonds.

Letter

Dear Morris,

I enjoyed sitting in on your afternoon production meeting yesterday. Your new procedure where each shift manager reviews individual production accounts for the next shift manager is working very well. For example, this month alone shows a 7 percent decrease in "do-overs."

We are now requiring certain departments to set up a turnover policy, starting with Proofreading and Agency Ads. Based on your experience, the supervisors in these two departments will be able to accomplish the turnover in 15 minutes, except in very rare instances.

Keep up the good work!

Best regards,

Congratulate Fellow Employee on Retirement

Situation

Patricia Brogden is retiring, and several of her friends write letters of congratulation to her. Each of them expresses a similar sentiment, that she was a good friend at work and will be missed. Her coworker Herb Ferguson writes the following letter.

Letter

Dear Patricia:

Congratulations on your retirement. You've been constantly pursuing new challenges during your years here at Watson-Ferguson, and I can't think of one that you didn't master. It's your fierce determination, tempered with a delightful wit, that has made you such an outstanding financial executive.

Your plans to take an Alaskan cruise sound like a lot more fun than tracking the bond market and dealing with security analysts. All of us here in the financial division will miss your expertise and good humor.

Here's wishing you many happy retirement years. Be sure to come back and see us now and again.

Best personal regards,

Congratulate Member of the Community

Situation

The owner of a small manufacturing company in a resort area learns that one of his customers has recently been elected president of the local Chamber of Commerce. The owner writes to extend his congratulations and offer support.

Letter

Dear Jules:

I just heard the good news that you are the new president of the Ocean Isles Chamber of Commerce. Congratulations!

The Chamber has done a remarkable job of attracting new industry, professional people, tourists, and retirees to this community. Now that you're president, I expect the Chamber to grow bigger and achieve more.

The Chamber has long had our support, and our resolve is now stronger than ever to contribute to its continued growth and success. Best wishes in this new post.

Sincerely,

Congratulations on Professional Achievement

Situation

Jayne Simpson, a food wholesaler, learns that one of her longtime customers has just been elected president of a retail food association. She keeps informed about people in her business by reading trade journals, then writes congratulatory messages to customers and friends who have received recognition.

Letter

Dear Curtis:

I was delighted to see in the September issue of *Food Retailer* that you have been named president of the Missouri Association of Independent Grocers. It was a pleasure to see this honor bestowed on a longtime friend and customer, and I know you will bring dynamic leadership to this important organization.

I extend hearty congratulations and good wishes. Our company is a longtime supporter of MAIG, so let me know if we can offer any assistance. We're behind you all the way!

Warmest regards,

Customer Takes Unearned Discount

Situation

Northwestern Housewares pays an invoice to Regal Plastics, but takes a discount to which the company is not entitled. The accounts receivable manager at Regal e-mails Northwestern's accounting department, explaining tactfully that money is still due on the invoice.

E-mail

Dear Mr. Lee:

Your check #1234 dated September 7 for $927.96 has been credited to your account. There is a balance due of $48.84.

Please note you are entitled to a 2 percent discount only if the invoice is paid within 10 days. Unfortunately you did not remit payment for 60 days.

Although we would like to make an exception in your case, such an action would penalize those who are given the same privilege. I understand that you enforce a similar policy in your organization.

Thank you for your cooperation in this matter.

Sincerely,

Damaged Shipment; Customer at Fault

Situation

Blue Dart Trucking is the carrier for a large furniture manufacturer, Stur-D, Inc. One of Stur-D's customers complains that a recent shipment of tables arrived with damage to several. The Blue Dart service manager looks into the matter and reports to Stur-D's claims manager.

Letter

Dear Clarence:

Our records show that all containers in shipment QRW57 were delivered on March 14 and accepted by R. P. Simpson. A copy of the waybill has already been faxed to you. Both Simpson and our driver signed off on this, so there was no evidence of damage to the outside of the boxes.

This suggests that either the tables were not packed properly for shipment—unlikely, since they came from your warehouse—or the tables were damaged while being unpacked.

Hope this information is helpful.

Best,

Damaged Shipment; Supplier at Fault

Situation

Clark Armend, director of the public library, placed an order with WonderBuilt Interiors for six carrels. The carrels were damaged when unpacked. Armend phoned WonderBuilt, and they promised to look into the problem. WonderBuilt now replies.

Letter

Dear Mr. Armend:

Thank you for letting us know about the damaged carrels you received. You said that four were damaged beyond repair, and the remaining two would need extensive refinishing. I have investigated this matter, and it appears that the fault is ours. I have already ordered a replacement shipment; you can expect delivery within 10 days.

Please hold on to the damaged carrels until our insurance representative can verify the damage. I'm very sorry about this incident, especially because I know how eager you are to complete the library renovation. I hope this problem has not caused you undue delay.

Sincerely,

Damaged Stock Returned for Credit

Situation

Edgewater Interiors has a policy of accepting returns within three months of the date of purchase. Adele Lawrence, a decorating consultant, returns 16 framed art reproductions that have been badly damaged. Edgewater Interiors refuses to give her credit because the prints are not in salable condition.

Letter

Dear Ms. Lawrence:

When I talked with you about returning the 16 reproductions in our Art Master series of prints, I said that our policy is to accept for full credit all items returned in salable condition.

The prints arrived today, and I was shocked at their condition. Obviously, they were stored in direct sunlight, for the pictures are faded and the canvas warped. What's more, the finish on the frames is cracked and peeling.

I'm sorry to disappoint you, but we cannot credit your account for these returns.

Yours truly,

Employee Request to Attend Convention

Situation   Beverly Byers, editor, wants to attend a convention of the food industry. She writes a memo, asking permission. At the same time, she uses the memo to sell the idea to her superior.

Memo

To: Adam Fitzpatrick

From: Beverly Byers

Subject: Food & Beverage Convention

Dear Adam:

I would like permission to attend the Food and Beverage Industry Convention in Chicago on March 12-16.

There has been a great deal of discussion in recent editorial meetings about publishing cookbooks, and clearly, there is much information to be gained at this convention. My main focus would be to scout for the company, looking specifically for trends in cooking and equipment, while at the same time searching for possible authors.

For example, Hawaii has been a hotbed of culinary experimentation, combining Japanese and Polynesian flavors and techniques. At this convention, renowned chef Issey Yokumani will be giving a lecture/demonstration, so the convention would be an excellent opportunity to approach him on behalf of New Paths Publishing.

I'm attaching a breakdown of estimated expenses. Thanks for considering this. I do think you'll agree that this is an important venue for us to explore.

Sincerely,

Express Appreciation for Past Support

Situation   Tyler Trenton, president of Trenton Lawn Care, has been in business for only a short time. On the third anniversary of the company's founding, Trenton writes a letter to loyal customers to thank them for their support.

Letter   Dear Mr. Vargas:

This month Trenton Lawn Care is celebrating its third anniversary. It's a wonderful occasion for us, and we're delighted with the progress we've made.

Yet we're fully aware that we grew and prospered only because we found great friends like you who gave us loyal support along the way. The future looks bright, and we want to acknowledge your contribution to this rosy outlook.

As a special thank you to loyal customers, we're offering a 15 percent discount on all weed and grub applications ordered this month. Please mention this letter when you place your order to be sure you receive this special anniversary discount.

Sincerely,

Express Thanks for Professional Favor

Situation

Lou Aldridge is production manager of a large printing plant. Last month Lou was falling behind schedule due to several large accounts with lengthy print runs. In order to meet the schedule, he subcontracted several of his smaller accounts to a colleague who owns a small print shop in the area. The schedule was met, customers were pleased, and Aldridge writes his colleague to say thanks.

Letter

Dear Jimmy:

I just wanted to say thanks for your help last month. Because you were able to handle three of my smaller accounts—McGuffrey Paints, Bozun's Brake Parts, and the Schneider Sailcloth catalog—I was able to meet my delivery schedule. Getting those accounts onto your press meant I could finally free up our fastest press for the Super Stores job. We delivered the ad inserts to the *Daily Record* with only 90 minutes to spare. Too close for comfort, but thanks to you, we did it.

Please extend my sincere appreciation to your team.

Very best wishes,

Extend Good Wishes to Retiring Employee

Situation

Edwin Millspaugh is retiring. His immediate supervisor, Priscilla Simpson, writes a letter to express her appreciation for past service and extend warm wishes for the future.

Letter

Dear Ed:

It's hard to believe that you've decided to retire early, but I want to congratulate you and express my appreciation.

You can look back with pride and satisfaction on your years here at Gemstrand. No one knows more about manufacturing cost control than you, and your keen mind has guided us in making intelligent decisions. You have been a valuable ally and friend.

We will certainly miss you, and I extend to you every good wish for health, happiness, and satisfaction in the years ahead.

Best wishes,

Follow-Up After Services Have Been Rendered

Situation

Shortly after Gold Medal Insurance Company ends its convention at the Outer Banks Conference Center, the special events manager writes a follow-up letter. Its purpose is to build goodwill and encourage Gold Medal Insurance to return for another convention.

Letter

Dear Mr. Watson:

I hope you were pleased with your experience at Outer Banks Conference Center and that all the participants returned home with pleasant memories of their stay here.

We have recently embarked on a major remodeling program and expect to be finished in another three months. We're adding a second indoor pool, three new tennis courts, and a steam room next to the sauna. We're also offering a full line of spa services to our clients.

We certainly enjoyed hosting Gold Medal Insurance employees, and we look forward to having you return next year. If there is anything you can suggest that will help us improve our accommodations or services, please let me know.

Cordially,

Follow-Up of Sales Call

Situation   Keith Dixon, sales representative for Maryland Wholesale Hardware, has just paid his first visit to Myra Bolton, owner of Bolton Lumber. Dixon follows up each sales call with a brief note to the customer.

Letter   Dear Myra:

It was good to meet you this afternoon and review Bolton Lumber's hardware offerings. I'm confident that your order with us will complete your line and bring more customers into your store.

Your order is already being processed, and you can expect the shipment to arrive no later than April 21. I've also asked our research department to forward information on preventing wood rot. Feel free to photocopy this material to use as free handouts to your customers.

I'll be back in Memphis the week of March 4 and look forward to seeing you then. In the meantime, feel free to call me at (800) 555-4567.

Best regards,

Follow-Up on Previous Order

Situation

Lombard Golf, Inc., a mail order distributor of golf equipment, receives a large number of orders for junior-sized golf clubs. These are often sent to an address other than the buyer's, and Lombard knows that the clubs are typically a gift to a young grandchild, niece, or nephew. Lombard maintains a database of these purchases, and after five years the sales department writes each customer, encouraging the purchase of standard-sized clubs.

Letter

Dear Mr. Heath:

Five years ago I had the pleasure of filling your order for a set of Pinnacle junior golf clubs. It occurred to me that the person using those clubs is now ready for a set of standard-sized clubs.

Here is a wonderful opportunity to acknowledge that special person in your life. Our Maxim line is an ideal set of adult-sized clubs for teens who play golf. Maxim clubs have a more flexible shaft, making it easier to drive the ball farther. These clubs are ideal for young men. We also recommend them for women of any age.

The holidays are upon us, and I'm enclosing our latest catalog. Be sure to check our Web site for special offers exclusive to online customers. Right now there are great savings on golfing accessories, including gloves, head covers, and weekend bags.

Order before December 10 and we can guarantee delivery on or before December 24 at no extra charge.

Sincerely,

Formal Invitation to Special Exhibit

Situation

Excello Illumination Company will be an exhibitor at a convention of the American Institute of Architects at the Cow Palace in San Francisco. The sales manager reserves space for the exhibit plus an adjoining conference room. The conference room will be converted into a mini-theater where a promotional movie will be shown continuously. A formal invitation is sent to all members of AIA.

Invitation

EXCELLO ILLUMINATION CORPORATION

Cordially invites you

to visit its exhibit at the AIA convention at

The Cow Palace

San Francisco, California

March 6 to 9, 2006

And to view an exciting new film

Light Up the World

at the theater adjoining the exhibit.

The film briefly traces the history of artificial illumination

and presents new innovations in the science of lighting.

It will be shown every hour from 9 a.m. to 5 p.m.

Follow-Up with Exhibit Visitor

Situation

Exhibitors often have logbooks for convention visitors to sign. Salespeople may also collect business cards so that they can follow up after the convention with these potential customers. Later a salesperson writes each visitor and encloses a promotion brochure prepared especially for the occasion. The letter and enclosure reestablishes contact with the visitors and reminds each of the company's name and product line.

Letter

Dear Mrs. Ramos:

Thank you for visiting our exhibit at the AIA convention in San Francisco. I hope you enjoyed our film *Light Up the World* and had a chance to look at our new lighting system on display in the booth.

We think our new system is one of the most exciting developments in lighting to come along in recent years. The 24-volt lighting draws only 2½ watts per lamp with a life expectancy of 50 years. We will customize it to your specific manufacturing or office needs. Our customers are reporting an annual savings of up to 17 percent on their lighting costs.

Enclosed is additional information on this low-energy lighting system. I expect to be in your area within the month and would like to discuss in detail ways that Excello Illumination can help you solve your lighting needs.

Sincerely,

Handling Special Request

A graduate student in communications writes the president of Wedemark Corporation. She is making a study of the history of corporate annual reports and requests a copy of each of Wedemark's reports for the past 15 years. Only three can be sent, but the president has a suggestion for getting access to the others.

Letter

Dear Ms. Demetri:

Your study of the history of annual reports sounds very challenging, and I'm pleased that you want Wedemark represented.

I'm enclosing copies of our last three annual reports. Although earlier reports are no longer available, we have stored them on microfilm. If you are in Minneapolis, you are welcome to visit us and spend as much time as you wish examining these films. Contact our company librarian, J. C. Schultz, and he will set up a carrel for you with viewing equipment.

I am sure your study will prove to be quite an ambitious one, but certainly useful to a large number of people.

Cordially yours,

Introduce New Sales Representative

Situation

Richard Brownley is a salesman for Revere Food Products, Inc. He has recently been promoted. His sales manager writes a letter to Brownley's customers, introducing his replacement.

Letter

Dear Jeff:

I am writing to introduce Milton Tarter to you. He is now representing Revere Food Products in your area, and you will be hearing from him regularly. Milton is replacing Richard Brownley, who has been promoted to manager of customer services.

Milton was our representative in Arkansas and Missouri and did an outstanding job there. We received many letters of appreciation from his customers, and I'm sure you will find him very knowledgeable.

Milton will be contacting you soon. You can reach him right away at (800) 555-4567.

Cordially,

Introduce New Senior Manager

Situation
The president of Butler International announces a new position and introduces the person chosen to fill it.

Announcement
Executive Bulletin 33
Office of the President

I am pleased to announce the appointment of Dr. Hannah R. Mancini to the position of Director of Long-Range Planning. Dr. Mancini comes to us from Martin & Ferrell Management Consultants where she worked with several Fortune 500 companies on their long-range planning needs. Dr. Mancini's responsibilities at Butler will relate to the functions of every division in the company; she will report directly to me.

Please join me in welcoming Dr. Hannah Mancini to Butler International. I have assured her that she will have your full cooperation as she develops our long-range goals for the coming decades.

Invitation to Join Organization

Situation

Troy Conley has just opened a new business, Far West Office Supplies. The local Chamber of Commerce contacts Conley, offering congratulations on his new business venture and encouraging him to join the Chamber.

Letter

Dear Mr. Conley:

Congratulations on the opening of your store, Far West Office Supplies. I know that local merchants and citizens are enthusiastic about your venture and are pleased to finally have a convenient source that can supply all their office needs.

I would like to invite you to join the Chamber of Commerce. This association of merchants offers a wealth of ideas, customer leads, and industry news to local businesses such as yours. Our "breakfast club" meets every Tuesday from 7 a.m. to 8 a.m. at Hobart's Eatery, and I would be honored if you could attend next week as my guest. This will give you a chance to meet other members and learn more about what we can do for you.

Look forward to seeing you then.

Cordially,

Invitation to Open House

The National Association of Home Economics Teachers is having its annual convention in Minneapolis on June 4–7. Sterling Mills, manufacturer of flour and other food products, has its main headquarters in Minneapolis. The director of educational relations invites each member of the association to an open house during the convention.

Letter

Dear Friend:

Sterling Mills, a proud sponsor of the National Association of Home Economics Teachers, is pleased to host a special open house during this year's annual convention in Minneapolis. It will be held Tuesday evening, June 5, from 5:30 p.m. to 9:30 p.m.

We'll have a buffet with open bar from 5:30 p.m. to 7 p.m., followed by a guided tour of our plant, with extra time in our famous test kitchens and recipe testing center.

We're only a short walk from your convention headquarters, but there will be courtesy shuttles to pick you up and return you to your hotel at the end of the tour. Full details are included in your registration packet.

If you are planning to attend the convention, please indicate on the enclosed card whether you are likely to attend the Sterling Mills Open House. This tour has been a big success in previous years, and we want to be ready to welcome you again.

Sincerely,

Invite Speaker; No Funds Available

Situation

A state organization of retired persons is looking for a keynote speaker for the group's annual conference. No funds are available to pay the speaker.

Letter

Dear Dr. Burdette:

The Ohio chapter of the Association of Seniors is holding its annual conference in Columbus on June 17-19. As you might guess, most of our discussions will focus on the important role that senior citizens can play in community affairs.

Would you be our keynote speaker for this conference? We are well acquainted with your excellent newspaper and magazine articles on the importance to older people of keeping involved. Your remarks would set the tone perfectly for our conference. We expect an attendance of 275 persons.

Although our limited treasury does not permit payment of fees or expenses, we are hoping that your interest in the issues facing the aging will be a sufficient incentive for you to be with us. We do expect media coverage of this event, and we will do our best to see that your speech is highlighted.

I look forward to hearing from you.

Sincerely,

Keeping in Touch with Past Customers

Situation

Maria Tonnesi is sales promotion manager of Fenwick Carpet Company. Tonnesi has created a database to track her customers— not only recent buyers, but those customers from past years whose carpeting might be showing signs of wear by now. She writes a sales promotion letter designed to keep these customers coming back to Fenwick.

Letter

Dear Mr. Black:

My records show that we installed industrial carpeting throughout your offices five years ago. Although the carpeting you selected should be okay for now, it will soon be time to think about replacing it.

Fenwick is now the exclusive distributors for WearsWell Industrial Flooring. We think this is the best industrial carpeting on the market today, and I would like to drop off a few samples for you to examine. You're welcome to use these as doormats at each entry. That is a good way to see for yourself how well this carpeting stands up to heavy-duty office traffic.

I'd like to stop by on Thursday morning, and I'll bring our three most popular colors with me. Do let me know if there is a specific color choice that interests you.

Cordially,

Making a Donation

A commencement speaker is paid an honorarium of $500, but chooses to donate the money to the university instead.

Letter

Dear Dr. Garvey:

You were very generous in your comments about my address at last week's commencement exercises, and I am most appreciative. It was an honor to participate.

Thank you for the honorarium of $500, but I would like to give this money to the university. Therefore, I am enclosing a personal check for $500 to be donated to the Leonard Moore Scholarship Fund.

Thank you for the many courtesies while I was in Miami. It was an experience that I'll long remember.

Sincerely,

Mistake in Filling Order

Situation

Clifford Sanford, owner of Trophy House, sells trophies of all kinds, including medals, plaques, cups, ribbons, and more. Customer Marvin Kallou orders 12 watches with a tennis motif, but instead receives watches with a golf motif. He phones Sanford, who immediately promises to rectify the mistake.

Letter

Dear Marvin:

Twelve Gemset watches with a tennis motif were sent today by Overnight Delivery Service to replace the watches you received in error. The mistake was ours and we apologize.

I also enclosed a box—complete with address label, return postage, and bubble wrap—so that you can return the golf watches. Just enclose the watches, tape the box shut, and drop it in the nearest mailbox.

Thanks for letting us know what happened. I am much relieved that you will have the correct watches in time for your awards banquet.

Cordially,

Notification of Delayed Shipment

Situation

The manufacturer of hospital uniforms and supplies received an order from Washaw General Hospital for 200 patient gowns in assorted sizes. The manufacturer notifies the hospital that a partial order has been shipped.

Letter

Dear Mr. Barrett:

Your order of July 14 has been processed. This letter is confirmation of shipping dates for the following items.

Order No.	Item No.	Description	Quantity	Ship Date	Expected Ship Date
WGH123456	4415MED	Patient gowns	50	July 19	
WGH123456	4415LG	Patient gowns	50	July 19	
WGH123456	4415XLG	Patient gowns	50	July 19	
WGH123456	4415XXLG	Patient gowns	50		July 23

Your order is shipped via Standard Delivery and should arrive in 7 to 10 days. To track your shipments online go to our Web site, or call our customer service department at (800) 555-4567.

Sincerely,

Notification of Item Out of Stock

Situation

Charles Devers, a clothing sales representative, has promised his smaller retail customers that they will receive their shipments of red, white, and blue baseball caps with a flag motif within two weeks. However, he soon learns that the manufacturer is out of stock due to the item's unexpected popularity. As a result, large orders to clothing chains are being filled first. Devers writes to his clients to apologize for the delay.

Letter

Dear Mrs. Maggard:

When your order was placed last week for 15 of the flag-motif baseball caps, I expected immediate shipment. However, as you no doubt know by now, there has been a run on these caps ever since rock-and-roll legend Ricky Rodriguez was seen wearing one at the All-Star Game.

Our inventory of these caps was more than adequate for the season, but no one could have foreseen this event. Needless to say, our manufacturers are working round the clock, but we expect at least a three-week delay before your order will be shipped.

I will assume that this unfortunate delay is acceptable to you. If you wish to change your order, either to cancel or increase it, please let me know by the end of this week. Call me at (800) 555-4567 and leave a message. I'll get back to you before the day is over.

Thanks for your patience in this matter.

Cordially,

Offer Alternate Source to Customer

Situation

Penelope Smith is looking for a specific book that is now out of print. She doesn't remember the title, but recalls the content quite clearly. She contacted a used book dealer, asking if he had this book in stock. The dealer writes to her, explaining that he no longer has the book she is looking for, but offers a suggestion for finding it elsewhere.

Letter

Dear Ms. Smith:

I have scoured our lists of out-of-print books very carefully, and I think I have a clue to the identity of the one you asked for. A book entitled *Practical Handbook of Mathematic Tables* by J. W. Shurz was published in 1919 by Eureka Publishing Company. The book went out of print in 1932, and the publisher is no longer in business. At one time I had a few copies, but unfortunately we have had none for several years.

There are many dealers throughout the country who specialize in rare and out-of-print books, and you may wish to contact some of them. I am attaching a list of three dealers whom I have found to be most reputable.

I wish you success in finding this treasure.

Cordially,

Offer Sympathy to Family of Coworker

Situation

Gary Gordon, a programming specialist, recently passed away after a long illness. One of his coworkers, Michael Ming, wrote a letter to Gordon's family to express his sympathy. Although the two men were not close friends, Ming wanted to share a pleasant memory with Gordon's family.

Letter

Dear Mrs. Gordon:

I was so sorry to learn that Gary had passed away. Although not totally unexpected, it is still quite sad.

Gary and I worked together on several projects at DynaCraw Electronics. He was always accessible and very knowledgeable about our industry, so it was a pleasure to work with him. Even when deadlines were upon us and we had already been working ridiculously long hours, Gary was upbeat and cheerful.

Please accept my condolences. I hope that good memories will help to ease the pain of his passing.

Sincerely,

Polite Turn-Down of Request to Donate

Situation

Most companies get many requests to make donations to various charities. Halpern Associates has a committee of officers to consider each request and allocate contributions to charities they feel would be best for the company to support.

Letter

Dear Mrs. Mueller:

We at Halpern Associates support various charities in the community, and we thank you for giving us the opportunity to consider donating to the Duprey Youth Symphony.

Although we feel that the youth symphony contributes much to the community, we are unable to provide financial support at this time.

In the meantime, we wish you success with your efforts on behalf of this excellent organization.

Sincerely,

Poor Service on Special Order

Situation

Lomack's, a retail gift shop, had placed a special order with a long-time supplier for monogrammed crystal stemware, but the order was not processed correctly. The owner of Lomack's calls the supplier to complain, then writes a letter to confirm their discussion.

Letter

Dear Martin:

It was good to talk to you this afternoon about the stemware problem, and I appreciate your help in resolving this issue. My customer was understandably quite upset.

1. Order #1234 was not fulfilled in a reasonable time. Instead of delivery in 5 business days, your standard policy, the order arrived in 17 business days.

2. The monogram was wrong. The order stated G in Old English. The glasses arrived with a C in block lettering.

3. Two of the wine glasses were broken.

Per our discussion, you will fulfill this order again, this time with the correct monogram. There will be no charge for shipping and handling. Delivery will be in three business days.

Thanks again for taking care of this matter.

Sincerely,

Reporting on Heavy Turnover in Regional Office

Situation

Tina Matthews is assistant sales manager of Hopewell Boxes, Inc. Recently she was asked by the sales manager to go to Richmond to investigate the heavy turnover of sales representatives in that region. Upon her return, she writes a report summarizing her findings.

Memo

To: Philip Terasaki

From: Tina Matthews

Subject: Richmond Report

Dear Phil:

I spent three days in Richmond last week. The problem is what you suspected—our compensation policy. I was able to contact all six reps who resigned during the past 18 months. Each spoke highly of our products and the company as a whole. In every instance, the overriding reason was money. All claimed big increases in income in their new jobs.

Also, the incentive plans based on increase in sales volume offered by other companies were a powerful inducement. Of the six who left, four went to McAllister, our toughest competitor in this area of the country.

I spent time with our current reps, and the subject of money came up constantly. Clearly, it's time to rework our salary/incentive program for the sales force. Let's set up a teleconference with three regional managers: Lamar King, Byllie Sherron, and Peter Rostenburg. They expressed a great deal of concern at last month's national sales conference, and I'm sure they'll have good input.

I've attached a spreadsheet comparing our compensation package with McAllister's. We can start with that. Like you, I'd very much like to get this matter resolved before we lose more sales staff.

Best,

Request More Information

Situation

Beckwirth Corporation has been reevaluating the company's benefit programs. Harold G. Slotkin, manager of human resources, recently attended a symposium on life insurance and was very interested in what the speaker had to say.

Letter

Dear Professor Strachan:

I enjoyed immensely your presentation on supplemental benefit plans at the AMA symposium on life insurance in San Francisco last week.

We are evaluating our voluntary benefits program here at Beckwith Corporation, and I know our Benefits Committee would find your ideas not only stimulating but also extremely helpful in our planning. Is a copy of your paper available? If so, I would like to reproduce it for distribution here.

Thank you for your consideration. I look forward to hearing from you.

Cordially,

Response to Employee's Report

Situation

Clarence Wainwright is a consulting engineer, and after extensive investigation, he proposes a new market for the company. When the marketing director reads this carefully researched report, he offers congratulations and emphasizes its importance to the company.

Letter

Dear Clarence:

I just read your report, "Energy Management—A New Market for Engineering Resources, Inc." Although I have been seeing some articles on this in the trade press recently, I did not realize that the demand for energy management was so explosive. Yet your report makes it clear that this is a logical development in a period of economic slowdown and escalating fuel costs.

I'd like for you to give a presentation to the sales and marketing committee on July 17. We'll be meeting in the Olympic Room at 9:30. Your conclusions and recommendations deserve careful consideration, and I have already forwarded copies of your report to committee members. Plan to stay after your presentation for the discussion that will follow.

Regards,

Response to Friendly Critic

Situation

International Technologies is a large conglomerate that sponsors a public service television series, *American Issues.* The public relations department answers letters from viewers who comment on various programs. The following letter is to a viewer who took issue with a recent segment on environmental issues.

Letter

Dear Professor Morrey:

Thank you for your recent letter about our television series, *American Issues.* Your comments on "Environment versus Progress" indicate that you have given much study and thought to this subject, and we appreciate your frank appraisal.

The producers were well aware that this is a highly controversial subject and were determined not to take sides. Our mail would seem to indicate that they succeeded. For every response saying that the program was biased in favor of the industrialists, we received an equal number who felt the bias was with the environmentalists.

Indeed, conflicting viewpoints are expected on this series, and as long as they are fairly well balanced, as they have been, we feel that the series is encouraging people to think more intelligently and deeply about the unresolved issues that face our nation.

Thank you for writing. We appreciate your interest in *American Issues.*

Sincerely,

Response to Outraged Critic

Situation

A large corporation receives a severely critical letter from the owner of a construction business. The writer is upset that the corporation is advertising in *Bulwark,* a magazine that the writer feels is "militant and un-American." The writer is incensed at the corporation's "support of this magazine" and he threatens to boycott its products. The head of the public relations department responds, tactfully explaining the company's position.

Letter

Dear Mr. Coughlin:

I appreciate your writing about our advertising in *Bulwark* magazine.

Bulwark was chosen as an advertising medium because its readership is mostly young men and women in certain age and income brackets. These are the readers whom we consider prime users of our products.

Placing advertising in a publication does not necessarily mean that we endorse its editorial views, and spending advertising dollars does not mean "support." Certainly we would never advertise in periodicals that are prurient in nature or that are essentially scandal sheets. Our media people place ads where they think our products will get the widest exposure to our customers, and in fact, most companies use the same criteria in choosing media.

Thank you for expressing your views so frankly and for giving us the opportunity to express ours.

Very truly yours,

Saying No to Request to Use Name

Kenneth Burton receives a letter from an organization called Parents for Library Censorship. This group wants to list Burton's name as a supporter on PLC stationery and other printed materials. Burton says no emphatically.

Letter

Dear Mr. Dennison,

I refuse permission for you to use my name as a supporter for your organization. Your goals are extremely offensive because they undermine free speech, one of our country's most important constitutional rights. I feel very strongly that no person or organization should take it upon themselves to determine what is "suitable" literature for other people.

I spoke out very strongly against library censorship at a recent town meeting, and I will continue to do so when the opportunity arises.

Again, I will not now or ever support your organization.

Yours truly,

Selling a Book

Situation

A publisher of college textbooks writes to university professors to whet their interest in purchasing a new book about Abraham Lincoln. Using mail-merge capabilities, each letter is personalized with the recipient's name.

Letter

Dear Dr. Kirchner:

Pathfinder Publishers is proud to announce the publication of *Abraham Lincoln: The Man and His Writings*. This is the most comprehensive selection of Abraham Lincoln's speeches, public writings, and private letters ever published. Lincoln was one of our greatest presidents, and in the opinion of many, one of the greatest writers ever to occupy the White House.

Each selection is introduced with an overview of the historical events that were the catalysts for Lincoln's writings. These overviews have been prepared by two renowned experts in American history, Dr. Vernon Langden and Dr. Lillian Streeter.

Here are all of Lincoln's speeches, from the early days in Illinois to his profoundly moving presidential speeches, including his inaugural addresses, the famous Gettysburg address, and his annual State of the Union messages to Congress.

Here too are the full texts of the stormy Lincoln-Douglas debates. Both Lincoln's and Douglas's own speeches are included, along with historical background from Knox College in Galesburg, Illinois, where the most famous of these debates occurred.

Here is Lincoln's personal political correspondence, including his satirical "Rebecca" letter that nearly lead to a duel, and his poignant letter to Mrs. Lydia Bixby upon hearing she had lost five sons in battle.

Here are Lincoln's war dispatches, his presidential messages and proclamations. Here are his poems and private reflections on democracy, slavery, and the meaning of the Civil War's immense suffering.

Above all, here is Lincoln's distinctive language, resonating with the dignity, wit, and uniquely American flavor of his Midwest origins.

Order your copy of *Abraham Lincoln: The Man and His Writings*. Today!

Selling a Consumer Product

Situation

A manufacturer of portable refrigerators purchases a mailing list of camping enthusiasts and sends a promotional piece in the form of a letter.

Letter

Dear Fellow Camper:

Traveling by car, camper, and van just got easier!

The new Lektron Kool portable refrigerator keeps drinks, sandwiches, and snacks at your fingertips. No more stops for expensive fast food. Prepare your own healthy meals, then stop and enjoy the view at scenic byways, away from traffic and crowds. You'll always be assured that the food is still fresh and the drinks are cold.

The Lektron Kool is a lightweight, roomy electric refrigerator that you can plug into your car, using a 110-volt adaptor that is included with the refrigerator. Lektron Kool's thermoelectric, solid-state motor replaces all the bulky piping coils and compressors found in conventional portable refrigerators.

Robert M., an enthusiastic owner of Lektron Kool, says, "Last summer our family took a month-long camping trip through Canada. The most important piece of equipment we carried was our Lektron Kool refrigerator. It was not only a convenience—it also saved us a bundle of cash!"

Now you can own the Lektron Kool for $50 less that the regular price. Order today! Call our toll-free number 800-555-LEKTRON, and be sure to mention code LK16A. If you order online at our Web site, you'll get the same discount by entering code LK16A under "special offers." As always, we have a generous 30-day return policy.

Remember, keep your food cool with a Lektron Kool refrigerator.

Sincerely,

Selling a Retirement Community

Situation

Sunset Harbor Village, a retirement community under construction, sends a promotion letter and brochure to a mailing list of people nearing retirement age.

Letter

Dear Mr. Logan:

Now that you are nearing retirement age, your golden years are just beginning. These are years that can be enriched beyond your dreams simply by moving to Sunset Harbor Village, a retirement community designed for people like you.

Sunset Harbor Village offers you the best life-care retirement living in a gracious new community just outside of Tulsa. You'll enjoy a private apartment, midday and evening gourmet meals in our private dining room, social and recreational activities. We also offer personal services such as our own beauty and barber shops, laundry, housekeeping, scheduled transportation, and round-the-clock health care, should you ever need it.

I would like to personally invite you to visit me at our information center so that I can show you the rewarding lifestyle that can be yours at Sunset Harbor Village. We're open from 9 a.m. to 5 p.m., Monday through Saturday, and noon to 4 p.m. on Sundays. Or, just give me a call to schedule a personal tour.

Sincerely,

Selling an Educational Course

Situation

Cameron Career Institute offers home-study courses in various trade occupations. The sales promotion director has purchased a mailing list of subscribers from several hobbyist magazines. These subscribers are often good candidates for home-study training. The following sales letter is designed to interest readers in a course in small-engine repair.

Letter

Would you like to own your own business?

If you're looking for the chance to be your own boss . . . or earn extra income in your spare time . . . or achieve independence when you retire . . . SMALL-ENGINE REPAIR could be the answer. It's a great way to get started with your own business with a minimum investment. Start part-time now, then grow your business into a full-time enterprise.

Cameron Career Institute (CCI) can quickly train you in your spare time to service and repair dozens of types of small-engine equipment—mowers, tillers, chain saws, outboard motors, garden tractors, motorcycles, snowmobiles, and more.

CCI's Small-Engine Repair course contains 45 lessons, each easy to read and understand. Every lesson is short and fully illustrated with step-by-step diagrams and photographs. It is hands-on training, too. You actually build a $3\frac{1}{2}$-horsepower four-cycle engine. With each lesson you will perform experiments that show you how every part of an engine works.

And, we supply you with professional tools! The course materials include a complete set of wrenches, electrical system tools, tachometer, engine overhaul tools, volt-ohm-milliamp meter, and all the miscellaneous nuts, bolts, and wires that you will need to complete each lesson.

The enclosed catalog has a detailed description of each lesson, shows sample pages of the study materials, and has pictures of the equipment you'll be using. Each student is assigned a personal instructor who is a professional small-engine mechanic with many years of experience. He will be your mentor as you work through your lessons.

Let us hear from you soon. We can help with financing arrangements, and in some cases, you may be eligible for veteran educational benefits. This is the opportunity you've been waiting for—and we're here to help you take advantage of it.

Sincerely,

Selling Conference Accommodations

Situation

A conference center manager sends a promotion letter to subscribers of *The Sales Executive*, inviting them to choose Whispering Pines Conference Center for their next meeting. A mail-merge program makes it possible to personalize each letter.

Letter

Dear Mr. Edwards:

Pardon us for bragging, but we just heard from the vice president of one of the country's largest manufacturing companies. Here's what he had to say: *"Thank you for helping us put on the best conference we've had yet. Your superb facilities, outstanding service, and knowledgeable suggestions added another layer of professionalism to our meetings."*

We at Whispering Pines pride ourselves in knowing how to help you make your meetings successful. It's why we're the ideal convention headquarters. We are first of all a magnificent resort center that offers all the amenities—outstanding cuisine, professional entertainment, indoor and outdoor swimming pools, tennis courts, boutique shopping, four tennis courts, and an 18-hole championship golf course.

Our staff of professional meeting planners will help you plan your next convention. Our multimedia conference rooms are ideal for presentations, and we can accommodate every size group from 5 to 500 attendees.

Please look over the enclosed booklet, which shows our elegant facilities. Then call our staff of professional meeting planners, and they will help you make complete arrangements for your next convention. If you return the enclosed card, we'll send you a free copy of *Making the Most of Your Multimedia Presentations*.

Sincerely,

Send Get Well Wishes

Situation

Myra Binders just learned that one of her staff members, Rick Laughlin, was injured in an automobile accident. Myra writes to wish him a speedy recovery.

Letter

Dear Rick:

I was shocked when I heard about your automobile accident. From what your wife said, it sounded dreadful, yet a miracle that your injuries weren't worse.

You're missed here, but I want to reassure you that while you're regaining your strength, we'll cover for you until you can return to work. Everyone in the department sends hearty get-well wishes.

Take care,

Suggest New Product

Situation   Vivian Keller, salesperson for an educational publisher, learns that one of her customers has ordered a book on filing. She contacts the customer and suggests an additional book that might be of interest.

Letter   Dear Ernest:

The book you ordered, *Filing and Finding*, is available, and six copies are already on the way to you.

I thought you might also be interested in our latest release, *Modern Records Management*. This new text covers the traditional methods of paper filing, but it focuses on the many new aspects of electronic record keeping. As you know, records management has undergone a dramatic revolution, triggered by the advances in computer and digital technology.

Many of my customers have found this new text exciting and highly informative. And best of all, they appreciate the supplementary teaching aids that are available with this text. Let me know if you'd like to learn more.

Cordially,

Thank Customer for Referral

Ralph Miller is the owner of Centennial Automotive Parts. One of Miller's longtime customers, Paul Harmon, has recommended his products to a friend. The result is a new customer and large order for Miller. He writes Harmon, thanking him for the referral.

Letter

Dear Paul:

Yesterday I received a large order from Binghamton Auto Supply and was told that your recommendation was important in my getting this business.

I was delighted to have the new business, but even more pleased that you thought well enough of Centennial Automotive Parts to recommend us to Binghamton. That's the highest compliment any business can receive, and I am grateful for it.

Many thanks,

Thank Speaker

Situation

Dr. Teresa Worth was asked to be the main speaker at a two-day workshop of the National Association of Manufacturing Managers. She did an outstanding job, and the program chairperson writes her a thank you letter.

Letter

Dear Teresa:

Thank you for being our keynote speaker at the recent NAMM conference. You set the perfect tone for the rest of the conference with your address, "Dynamic Manufacturing Management." I heard three panel discussions the next day and was pleased to hear several references to your talk. You obviously widened the perspective of all our members.

Thanks again for participating so effectively in our national conference. You played a major role in making it an outstanding event.

Sincerely,

Thank Supplier

Situation

Lazarus Brothers Company is a manufacturer of fine furniture. Most of their raw materials are delivered by truck. During a recent truckers' strike, the company was forced to slow down production. One of their suppliers was able to deliver materials via other means, and the president of Lazarus Brothers writes to express his appreciation.

Letter

Dear Mr. Rambeau:

All of us at Lazarus Brothers have been highly pleased with the excellent service you gave us during the truckers' strike. The situation called for great inventiveness on your part to see that we got the materials we needed. I understand that we were one of very few companies in this area who didn't have to shut down because of lack of materials.

On behalf of everyone here I want to express sincere appreciation for your performance during this difficult period. Thanks again.

Best regards,

Turn Down Opportunity to Buy Advertising

Situation

Tyllson Togs sells sports uniforms and equipment for high schools and colleges. Every year, the company receives letters from yearbook editors asking them to place ads in the yearbooks. Since the people who read these ads are the local residents, Tyllson turns down these requests.

Letter

Dear Ms. Schaefer:

Thank you for your invitation to purchase an ad in your yearbook. Unfortunately, we must decline this opportunity.

Our experience suggests that you will have to rely primarily on local community businesses to purchase ads in *Reminiscence*. Many businesses feel a strong obligation to support worthy community activities in their area, and just having their names associated with an annual school publication is a strong incentive.

Thank you for thinking of us, and we extend our best wishes for a successful yearbook.

Cordially,

Unauthorized Return of Merchandise

Situation

Cabrizzi's Building Supply returns 34 gallons of paint to the manufacturer and asks for full credit. This brand has been discontinued, and all dealers were notified. The manufacturer denies the request, but offers a compromise.

Letter

Dear Mr. Cabrizzi:

We have received the 34 one-gallon cans of exterior white Dura-Glow paint you returned. Unfortunately, we cannot allow you full credit on this paint. You were notified, along with all other dealers, that this line was being discontinued and that we would only accept returns through September of last year. It is now 14 months after that date.

We can, however, do this—we have credited your account for $4.75 per gallon. The difference is the cost to us to dispose of the paint.

Luxor Sheen paints have replaced the Dura-Glow line. Dealers are delighted with consumer acceptance of the Luxor paints, and most are reporting an increase in sales with this line. I'm enclosing a price list and color samples for you to look over. We'd be happy to have an order from you.

Sincerely,

Unauthorized Use of Service Personnel

Situation

Dykstron Computers has service contracts with many of the firms that use the company's equipment. These contracts stipulate that the company will provide service on Dykstron computers only. It comes to the service manager's attention that at one place of business, Dykstron technicians are being asked to service other brands. The service manager wants to stop this practice.

Letter

Dear Mr. Murphy:

As you know, our contract with you stipulates that we will provide services to all Dykstron equipment. I hope you feel that our service so far has been prompt and professional in every respect.

Recently our technicians report that they have been asked by some of your supervisors to service equipment other than our own. In several instances our technicians actually did the work. I have asked them to decline any future requests for two reasons. First, our technicians are not always familiar with the specifics of other manufacturers' computers, and second, we do not want to assume responsibility for incorrect maintenance on equipment other than our own.

I suspect that you are unaware of this situation, but I felt you would want to know about it. I'm sure you'll agree that it can cause unnecessary problems for both of us. Thanks for your help in resolving this matter.

Sincerely,

Welcome New Resident

In small towns and suburban areas new residents are of special interest to retail stores. Often these newcomers are welcomed to the community with a personal letter. Mr. and Mrs. George Bryson and their three young children have recently moved to Springdale and receive a welcome letter from a local clothing store.

Dear Mr. and Mrs. Bryson:

We are delighted to welcome you to Springdale, and we are glad you chose our community to live in. We are proud of our schools and are confident your children will grow and thrive in our educational system.

For over 25 years Walton Family Clothiers has been Springdale's favorite shopping place for women's, men's, and children's wear. We feature popular brands, a complete range of sizes, and all coordinating accessories from shoes to hair ribbons. We accept all major credit cards.

Please stop by to say hello. We'd like to meet you and present your family with a special gift. Just bring this letter with you.

We hope you'll like living in Springdale. Springdale is small in size but large in friendliness.

Sincerely,

Win Back Inactive Customer

Situation

Hoffstedder Sporting Goods maintains a database of customers. They regularly offer special sales incentives to customers who have not purchased any merchandise recently. Hoffstedder sends each of these customers a personalized letter along with a coupon for a special sale.

Letter

Dear Mr. Evans:

We've had the happy experience of keeping you supplied with sports equipment in past years. Since we haven't seen you lately, we're offering a special enticement to encourage you to come by and say hello.

We're enclosing a coupon for a 10 percent discount on your next purchase. You can use this for items already on sale, too. Right now, all Hi-Flite hang gliders are reduced 25 percent over last year's prices. With your discount coupon, you can save up to 35 percent. This is the time to purchase that Hi-Flite you've been dreaming about and soar aloft.

If you want to stay on the ground, take a look at our Bashem tennis gear. All Bashem rackets are reduced 20 percent this week. Use the enclosed coupon for a total savings of 30 percent.

There are more bargains in the store. Take advantage of this special offer and get ready for the summer sports season.

Cordially,

Write Confirmation Memo

Brent Walker and Curtis Taylor recently met to discuss several changes in the Sales Training Department. Taylor, the department manager, approved the changes, and Walker writes to confirm the new changes.

To: Curtis Taylor

From: Brent Walker

Subject: Meeting Notes

Dear Curtis:

This will confirm our discussion Thursday in which we agreed on the following:

1. I am authorized to hire two staff members—an instructor and a multimedia specialist, effective August 1, at a total annual salary not to exceed $78,000. Allocation depends on the qualifications of the people hired. Arlene Fogerty in Human Resources will handle the initial screening of applicants.

2. My department has one available cubicle. I am authorized to have one more installed along with the usual equipment (furniture, file cabinet, computer, supplies, etc).

3. Hugh Hansfield will be promoted to Sales Intern Supervisor, also effective August 1, at a 5 percent salary increase. Assuming he accepts the promotion, I will prepare an announcement for your signature.

If you have any questions or want further clarification on these points, let me know. Otherwise, I will assume that we are in agreement on everything mentioned.

Regards,

Wrong Merchandise Sent

Situation

David Fitzhugh, owner of Southport Marina, orders eight outboard motors. Due to errors from both Fitzhugh and the manufacturer, the dealer is shipped motors that he doesn't want. Northeast Boating contacts Fitzhugh to clarify the matter.

Letter

Dear Mr. Fitzhugh:

I've investigated the problem with your order of eight 6-hp Sea Serpent outboard motors dated May 4. You received 7.5-hp motors instead.

Your order (photocopy enclosed) lists the 7.5-hp motor and stock number, but the price you include is for the 6-hp motor. We assumed that the stock number was correct, so we shipped it. We should have checked with you first, and I'm sorry we didn't.

The shipment of eight 6-hp motors has now been processed. You can expect to receive them no later than next Wednesday.

As you know, the 7.5-hp motor is also a big seller in the Sea Serpent line. I'd suggest that you keep them for 30 days, and if they don't move, then return them to us.

Sincerely,

Wrong Size Shipped Twice

Situation

Sidney Reilly is assistant sales manager for Mid-Continent Distributors, Inc. A building supply dealer, Beth Silver, is a longtime customer. She places an order for six 48-inch ceiling fans. The fans she receives are 36 inches. When the mistake is discovered, a second shipment is made, but this time she receives 56-inch fans. Silver makes an angry phone call. Reilly apologizes, sends a salesman to make a personal delivery of the correct size fans, then writes a follow-up letter. He hopes to mollify Silver and retain her as a loyal customer.

Letter

Dear Beth:

Six 48-inch Victory fans are on their way to you by messenger. Our sales representative, Andy Mathieson, will pick them up at our warehouse and deliver them personally tomorrow.

It's embarrassing to inconvenience any customer, especially one so highly valued as you. Please accept my sincere apologies. To help rectify this error, I've billed these fans to you at a 20 percent discount as a thank you for your understanding and patience.

We value your business and look forward to serving you better next time.

Best regards,

Index